Editors
Kim Fields
Sara Connol

Managing Editor
Ina Massler Levin, M.A.

Illustrator
Howard Cheney

Cover Artist
Courtney Barnes

Art Coordinator
Renée Christine Yates

Art Production Manager
Kevin Barnes

Imaging
Rosa C. See
Leonard P. Swierski

Publisher

Mary D. Smith, M.S. Ed.

NONFICTION READING COMPREHENSION

Informational Reading

Grades 1–2

Ideal for Test Practice

Includes Standards & Benchmarks

FIRE
PUSH IN THEN
PULL ▼ DOWN
NOTIFIER

Author

Tracie Heskett, M.Ed.

Teacher Created Resources, Inc.
6421 Industry Way
Westminster, CA 92683
www.teachercreated.com
ISBN: 978-1-4206-8861-0
© 2007 Teacher Created Resources, Inc.
Made in U.S.A.

Teacher Created Resources

Table of Contents

Introduction

Reading comprehension can be practiced and improved in the context of informational reading, as well as in the reading students do in the course of their daily lives. This book presents environmental print in the context of scenes and other print media, along with short stories of explanation. The topics chosen include familiar settings and experiences while at the same time introducing new vocabulary and ideas.

A page of questions follows each story. These questions will provide a child familiarity with different types of test questions. In addition, the practice they provide will help a child develop good testing skills. Questions are written so that they lead a child to focus on what was read. They provide practice for finding the main idea, as well as specific details. They provide practice in deciphering new and unknown vocabulary words. In addition, the questions encourage a child to think beyond the facts. For example, every question set has an analogy question where students are expected to think about the relationship between two things and find a pair of words with the same type of relationship. Other questions provide an opportunity for the child to infer and consider possible consequences relevant to the information provided in the story.

The book is designed so that writing can be incorporated into every lesson. The level of writing will depend on what the teacher desires, as well as the needs of the child.

Lessons in *Nonfiction Reading Comprehension: Informational Reading* meet and are correlated to the Mid-continent Research for Education and Learning (McRel) standards. They are listed on page 8.

A place for *Nonfiction Reading Comprehension: Informational Reading* can be found in every classroom or home. It can be a part of daily instruction in time designated for reading or other academic areas as specific topics of study relate to the stories presented. It can be used for both group and individual instruction. Stories can be read with someone or on one's own. *Nonfiction Reading Comprehension: Informational Reading* can help children improve in multiple areas, including reading, critical thinking, writing, and test-taking.

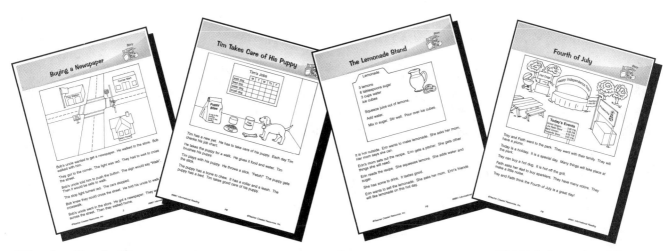

Using This Book *(cont.)*

The Stories

Each story in *Nonfiction Reading Comprehension: Informational Reading* is a separate unit. For this reason, the stories can be (but do not have to be) read in order. A teacher can choose any story that coincides with classroom activity.

Stories can be assigned to be read during reading or other related academic periods. They can be used as classroom work or supplemental material.

Each story contains a scene or sample of environmental print, as well as a short story of explanation. The stories range from 50 to 200 words in length. They are written at the first grade level and have elementary sentence structure.

New Words

Each story includes a list of eight vocabulary words. These words may be used in the short story or the environmental scene. New words may sometimes have an addition of a simple word ending such as s, ed, or ing. Many of the new words are found in more than one story. Mastery of the new words may not come immediately, but practice articulating, seeing, and writing the words will build a foundation for future learning.

❋ A teacher may choose to have the children read and repeat the words together as a class.

❋ While it is true that the majority of the words are defined explicitly or in context in the stories, a teacher may choose to discuss and define the new words before the students begin reading. This will only reinforce word identification and reading vocabulary.

❋ A teacher may engage the class in an activity where children use the new word in a sentence. Or, the teacher may use the word in two sentences. Only one sentence will use the word correctly. Children will be asked to identify which sentence is correct. For example, one new word is concert. The teacher might say,

"They listened to a band *concert*."

"He entered a *concert* and won a prize."

❋ A teacher may also allow children to choose one new word to add to their weekly spelling list. This provides children with an opportunity to feel part of a decision-making process, as well as to gain "ownership" over new words. In addition, practice spelling words reinforces the idea that we can learn to recognize new words across stories because there is consistency in spelling.

❋ A teacher may choose to have children go through the story after it is read and circle each new word.

Using This Book (cont.)

The Writing Link

✳ A teacher may choose to link writing exercises to the stories presented in the book. All writing links reinforce handwriting and spelling skills. Writing links with optional sentence tasks reinforce sentence construction and punctuation.

✳ A teacher may choose to have a child pick one new word from the list of new words and write it. Space for the word write-out is provided in this book. This option may seem simple, but it provides a child with an opportunity to take control. The child is not overwhelmed by the task of the word write-out because the child is choosing the word. It also reinforces word identification. If a teacher has begun to instruct children in cursive writing, the teacher can ask the child to write out the word twice: once in print, and once in cursive.

✳ A teacher may choose to have a child write a complete sentence using one of the new words. The sentences can be formulated together as a class or as individual work. Depending on other classroom work, the teacher may want to remind children about uppercase letters and ending punctuation.

✳ A teacher may require a child to write a sentence after the story questions have been answered. The sentence may or may not contain a new word. The sentence may have one of the following beginnings:

I learned . . . .   Did you know . . . ?

I thought . . . .   An interesting thing about . . . .

If a teacher decides on this type of sentence formation, he or she may want to show children how they can use words directly from the story to help form their sentences, as well as make sure that words in their sentences are not misspelled. For example, this is the first paragraph in the selection titled "June Fun."

A calendar shows what day it is. Lynn's mom has a calendar. She writes events on it.

Possible sample sentence write-outs:

"I learned that you can write events on a calendar."

"I thought that you used a calendar in the kitchen."

"Did you know a calendar shows the days?"

"An interesting thing about calendars is that you can write on them."

This type of exercise reinforces spelling and sentence structure. It also teaches a child responsibility: a child learns to go back to the story to check word spelling. It also provides elementary report-writing skills. Students are taking information from a story source and reporting it in their own sentence construction.

Using This Book (cont.)

The Questions

Five questions follow each story. Questions always contain one main-idea, specific-detail, and analogy question.

* The main-idea question pushes a child to focus on the topic of what was read. It allows practice in discerning between answers that are too broad or narrow.

* The specific-detail question requires a child to retrieve or recall a particular fact mentioned in the story. Children gain practice referring back to a source. They also are pushed to think about the structure of the story. Where would this fact most likely be mentioned in the story? What paragraph or part of the scene would most likely contain the fact to be retrieved?

* The analogy question pushes a child to develop reasoning skills. It pairs two words mentioned in the story or scene and asks the child to think about how the words relate to each other. A child is then asked to find an analogous pair. Children are expected to recognize and use analogies in all course readings, written work, and listening. This particular type of question is found on many cognitive-functioning tests.

The remaining two questions are a mixture of vocabulary, inference, identifying what is true or not true, or sequencing questions. Going back and reading the word in context can help answer vocabulary questions. The inference and sequencing questions provide practice for what students will find on standardized tests. They also encourage a child to think beyond the story. They allow a child to think critically about how facts can be interpreted.

The Test Link

Standardized tests have become obligatory in schools throughout our nation and the world. There are certain test-taking skills and strategies that can be developed by using *Nonfiction Reading Comprehension: Informational Reading*.

* Students can answer questions on the page by filling in the correct bubble, or you may choose to have your students use the provided answer sheet (page 141). Filling in the bubble page allows students to practice responding in a standardized-test format.

* Questions are presented in a mixed-up order, though the main-idea question is always among the first three questions. The analogy question is always one of the last three questions. This mixed-up order gives students practice with standardized test formats, but these types of questions are not necessarily placed first.

The Test Link *(cont.)*

✻ A teacher may want to point out to students that often a main-idea question can be used to help a child focus on what the story is about. A teacher may also want to point out that an analogy question can be done any time since it is not crucial to the main focus of the story.

✻ A teacher may want to remind students to read every answer choice. Many children are afraid of not remembering information. Reinforcing this tip helps a child remember that on multiple-choice tests, one is identifying the best answer—not making an answer up.

✻ A teacher may choose to discuss the strategy of eliminating wrong answer choices to find the correct one. Teachers should instruct children that even if they can only eliminate one answer choice, their guess would have a better chance of being correct. A teacher may want to go through several questions to demonstrate this strategy. For example, in the story scene "Seth's Lunch," there is the following question:

---

3. This story is mainly about

   Ⓐ how to eat chicken

   Ⓑ going to the restroom

   Ⓒ going to a restaurant

   Ⓓ how to be a king

Although chicken, restroom, and restaurant are mentioned in the story, there is no mention of a king. A child may be able to eliminate that answer choice immediately. A guess at this point has a better chance of being correct than when there were four choices to choose from. A teacher can also remind children that there is the option of going back and finding the parts of the scene with the words *chicken, restroom,* and *restaurant* in them. The scene shows the interior of a restaurant and describes Seth's experience there; *chicken* and *restroom* refer to minor points in the story. In fact, they appear to have equal weight. As one cannot be a better choice than the other, neither one of them can be correct.

Environmental Print

The term *environmental print* refers to the "printed words children see every day in the world around them." These words may be on signs, posters, containers, or buildings. Children read environmental print at home, in the classroom, stores, other places in the community, and outdoors. They also encounter print on a regular basis on directions, maps, and various types of schedules. Children become familiar with the words they see every day and can often read much more than others realize. Practice reading for information in various formats allows children to gain confidence in their reading comprehension and test-taking abilities as they encounter print with which they are already familiar.

Meeting Standards

Listed below are the McREL standards for Language Arts Level 1 (grades K–2). All standards and benchmarks are used with permission from McREL.

Copyright 2004 McREL

Mid-continent Research for Education and Learning

2550 S. Parker Road, Suite 500

Aurora, CO 80014

Telephone: (303) 337-0990

Website: *www.mcrel.org/standards-benchmarks*

McREL Standards are in **bold**. Benchmarks are in regular print. All lessons meet the following standards and benchmarks unless noted.

> **Uses grammatical and mechanical conventions in written compositions.**

* Uses conventions of print in writing (all lessons where writing a new word or sentence option is followed)

* Uses complete sentences in written compositions (all lessons where writing a complete sentence option is followed)

> **Uses the general skills and strategies of the reading process.**

* Understands that print conveys meaning

* Understands how print is organized and read

* Creates mental images from pictures and print

* Uses meaning clues

* Uses basic elements of phonetic analysis

* Uses basic elements of structural analysis

* Understands level-appropriate sight words and vocabulary

* Uses self-correction strategies

> **Uses reading skills and strategies to understand a variety of informational texts.**

* Uses reading skills and strategies to understand a variety of informational texts (e.g., written directions, signs, captions, warning labels, informational books)

* Understands the main idea and supporting details of simple expository information

Kala Helps Her Mom

These are new words to practice.
Say each word 10 times.

✳ produce   ✳ open

✳ grocery   ✳ checkout

✳ store   ✳ push

✳ pull   ✳ close

Choose one new word to write.

_____

- - - - - - - - - - - - - - - - - - -

_____

Kala Helps Her Mom

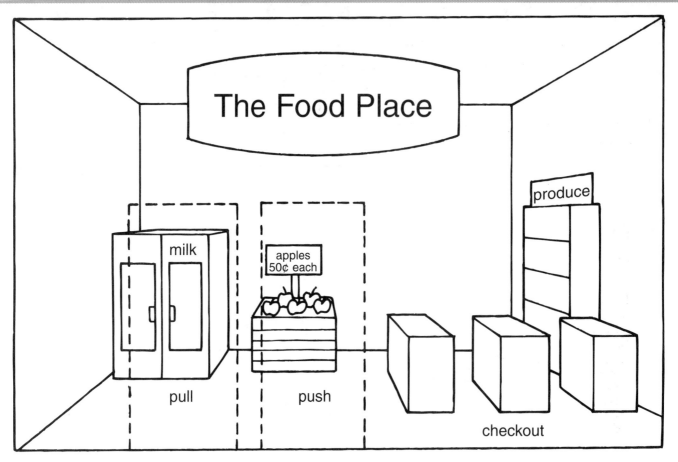

Kala went to the grocery store. She went with her mom. They walked into the store.

Kala saw a sign on the door. The sign said "pull." She pulled the door. The door opened.

Kala's mom got apples. She also got milk. She went to the checkout stand. Kala's mom paid for the food.

They left the store. Kala pushed the door open for her mom. The door closed behind them. Kala likes to help her mom buy food.

Kala Helps Her Mom

**Look at the picture on page 10. Read the story.
Use the picture and the story to answer the questions.**

1. How much money would Kala need to buy one apple?

   Ⓐ 25¢

   Ⓑ 30¢

   Ⓒ 50¢

   Ⓓ 80¢

2. This story is mostly about

   Ⓐ going to the grocery store

   Ⓑ a trip to the farm

   Ⓒ how to walk into a store

   Ⓓ how to eat apples

3. Think about how the word *push* relates to the word *pull*. Which words relate in the same way?

push : pull

   Ⓐ apples : milk

   Ⓑ sign : door

   Ⓒ open : close

   Ⓓ food : store

4. Where might Kala's mom find the milk?

   Ⓐ at the front of the store

   Ⓑ next to the apples

   Ⓒ by the checkout

   Ⓓ at the back of the store

5. Why did Kala's mom go to the checkout stand?

   Ⓐ to check out a book

   Ⓑ to pay for the food

   Ⓒ to ask a question

   Ⓓ to get apples

Buying a Newspaper

These are new words to practice.

Say each word 10 times.

✳ uncle   ✳ button

✳ newspaper   ✳ stop light

✳ walk   ✳ across

✳ wait   ✳ crosswalk

Choose one new word to write.

_____

- - - - - - - - - - - - - - - - -

_____

Buying a Newspaper

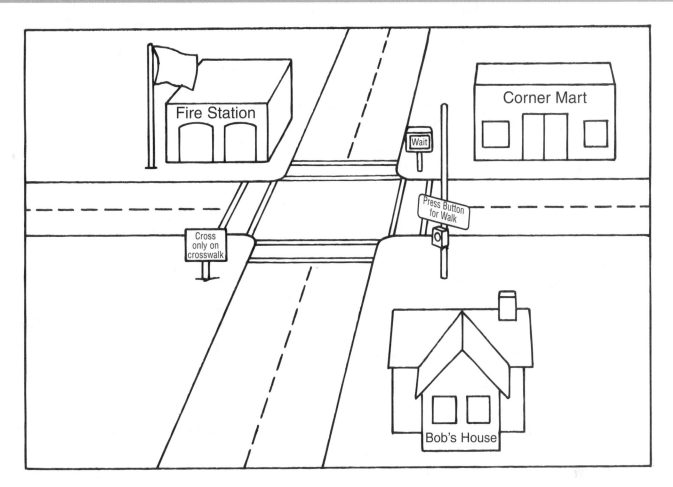

Bob's uncle wanted to get a newspaper. He walked to the store. Bob walked with him.

They got to the corner. The light was red. They had to wait to cross the street.

Bob's uncle told him to push the button. The sign would say "Walk." Then it would be safe to walk.

The stop light turned red. The cars stopped.

Bob knew they could cross the street. He told his uncle to walk in the crosswalk.

Bob's uncle went in the store. He got a newspaper. They waited to go across the street. Then they walked home.

Buying a Newspaper

Look at the picture on page 13. Read the story.

Use the picture and the story to answer the questions.

1. Bob and his uncle left the house. They wanted to go to the store. They needed to walk:

   (A) left

   (B) right

   (C) straight

   (D) left, then right

2. A *crosswalk* shows people

   (A) where they may safely cross the street

   (B) how to walk sideways

   (C) how to write an X

   (D) how to walk across the playground

3. This story is mainly about

   (A) Bob and his uncle

   (B) how to buy a newspaper

   (C) going to the fire station

   (D) how to cross the street safely

4. Why did Bob and his uncle want to cross the street?

   (A) so they could push the button

   (B) to get to the store

   (C) so they could walk

   (D) to go to the fire station

5. Think about how the word *walk* relates to *wait*. Which words relate in the same way?

walk : wait

   (A) go : stop

   (B) run : push

   (C) yellow : red

   (D) street : sign

Seth's Lunch

These are new words to practice.

Say each word 10 times.

* order   * nuggets

* menu   * men

* meal   * women

* value   * counter

Choose one new word to write.

_____

- -

_____

Seth's Lunch

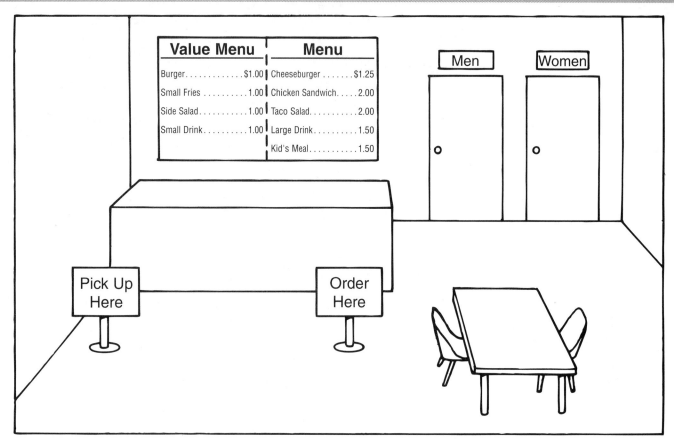

One day Seth went to Bill's Burgers. He went with his mom and dad. They wanted to have lunch.

Seth's dad parked the car. They walked inside.

Seth went to the counter. Seth ordered the kid's meal. He chose chicken nuggets. He wanted soda to drink.

Seth's dad ordered a chicken sandwich. He also had a large drink. Seth's mom was not hungry. She asked for a side salad.

They waited for their food. Seth's dad told him to wash his hands before lunch. They found a place to sit. Seth looked out the window.

A man called their number. Seth helped his dad get the food. They went to the pick-up line. Seth's family enjoyed their lunch.

Seth's Lunch

Look at the picture on page 16. Read the story.

Use the picture and the story to answer the questions.

1. How much did Seth's lunch cost?

   (A) $2.50

   (B) $1.50

   (C) $3.00

   (D) $2.00

2. Seth and his parents had lunch at

   (A) a grocery store

   (B) a house

   (C) a park

   (D) a restaurant

3. This story is mainly about

   (A) how to eat chicken

   (B) going to the restroom

   (C) going to a restaurant

   (D) how to be a king

4. Think about how the word *men* relates to *women*. Which words relate in the same way?

men : women

   (A) value : menu

   (B) burger : fries

   (C) women : ladies

   (D) dads : moms

5. Seth's family got their food

   (A) in the pick up line

   (B) in the order line

   (C) in the drive up line

   (D) by the door

Sam Goes Shopping

These are new words to practice.

Say each word 10 times.

✳ exit   ✳ broken

✳ enter   ✳ return

✳ sale   ✳ customer

✳ exchange   ✳ caution

Choose one new word to write.

_____

- -

_____

        18

Sam Goes Shopping

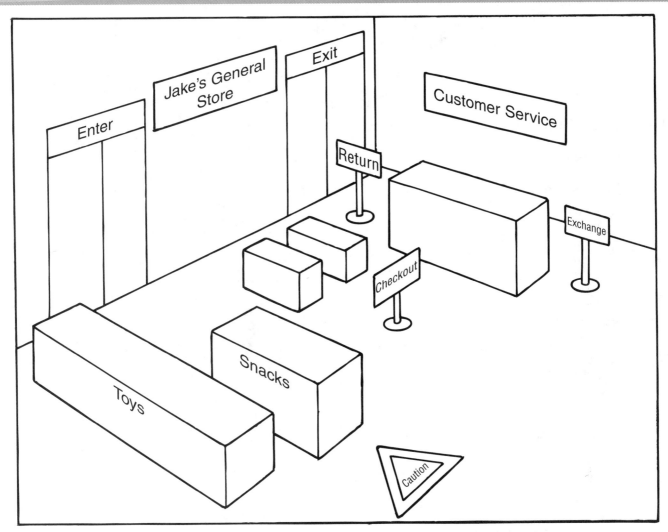

Sam has a toy. He got it for his birthday. The toy does not have one part.

Sam went to the store. He wanted to get a new toy. He will take back the broken toy.

In the store Sam saw a sign. The yellow sign was on the wet floor. Sam walked around the sign.

Sam found another toy. He exchanged the broken toy. Sam is happy to have a new toy.

Sam Goes Shopping

Look at the picture on page 19. Read the story.

Use the picture and the story to answer the questions.

1. The yellow *caution* sign means

   Ⓐ wet floor

   Ⓑ be careful

   Ⓒ walk here

   Ⓓ be happy

2. Sam can look at toys

   Ⓐ at the front of the store

   Ⓑ at the right side of the store

   Ⓒ at the left side of the store

   Ⓓ at the back of the store

3. The main idea of this scene is

   Ⓐ buying a toy

   Ⓑ washing the floor

   Ⓒ spending money

   Ⓓ finding your way in a store

4. Think about how the word *enter* relates to *exit*. Which words relate in the same way?

enter : exit

   Ⓐ in : out

   Ⓑ walk : go

   Ⓒ toys : candy

   Ⓓ wet : floor

5. Sam's toy broke. He wants to exchange it. He could

   Ⓐ go to the exit

   Ⓑ go to customer service

   Ⓒ go to the checkout stand

   Ⓓ go to the toys

Snack Time

These are new words to practice.

Say each word 10 times.

* ❋ hand cleanser ❋ cup

* ❋ snack ❋ helper

* ❋ ready ❋ napkin

* ❋ pour ❋ piece

Choose one new word to write.

_____

- - - - - - - - - - - - - - - - - - - -

_____

Snack Time

Beth's class has snack each day. Everyone must wash his or her hands. They sit in their chairs.

Mrs. Brown gets snack ready. Each child gets a cup. The teacher pours juice.

Today's helper hands out napkins. Mrs. Brown cuts apples. Each child has a piece of apple.

The children eat their apples. Yum! Beth likes snack time.

Snack Time

Look at the picture on page 22. Read the story.

Use the picture and the story to answer the questions.

1. With the apples, Beth's class could have

   (A) green beans

   (B) crackers

   (C) pizza

   (D) no snack

2. This story scene is mainly about

   (A) how to wash your hands

   (B) lunch

   (C) spelling

   (D) snack time

3. Think about how the word *juice* relates to *milk*. Which words relate in the same way?

juice : milk

   (A) snack : grapes

   (B) lunch : math

   (C) crackers : cereal

   (D) apples : green

4. To wash her hands, Beth used

   (A) hand cleanser

   (B) soap

   (C) the bathroom

   (D) a washcloth

5. When Mrs. Brown *poured* juice

   (A) she put the juice up

   (B) she put juice in a cup

   (C) it rained juice outside

   (D) the juice spilled quickly

Hana Goes to the Dentist

These are new words to practice.

Say each word 10 times.

✳ hours   ✳ doctor

✳ closed   ✳ patient

✳ dentist   ✳ office

✳ appointment   ✳ toothbrush

Choose one new word to write.

_____

- -

_____

Hana Goes to the Dentist

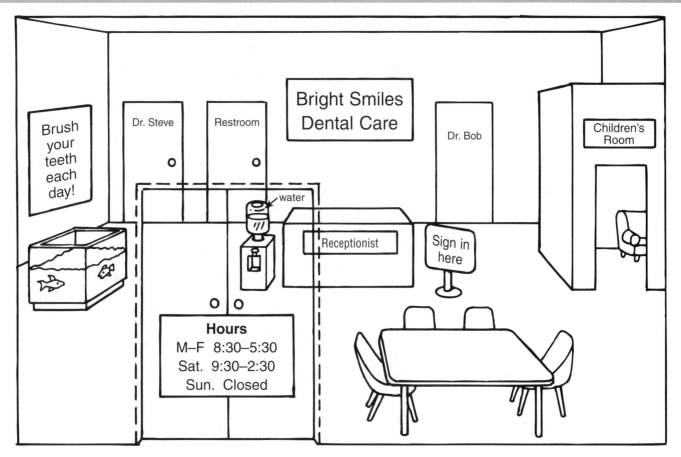

Hana is going to the dentist. She has an appointment. She will see Dr. Steve. Hana is his patient.

Hana waits in the office. She gets a drink of water. Someone calls her name.

Dr. Steve will check her teeth. He tells her to brush her teeth. She should use a toothbrush each day.

Hana Goes to the Dentist

Look at the picture on page 25. Read the story.

Use the picture and the story to answer the questions.

1. To see the dentist, Hana needs

   Ⓐ an appointment

   Ⓑ a patient

   Ⓒ an office

   Ⓓ a toothbrush

2. This scene is mainly about

   Ⓐ Steve and Bob

   Ⓑ going to the dentist

   Ⓒ going to the doctor

   Ⓓ watching a fish tank

3. Think about how the word *brush* relates to the word *teeth*. Which words relate in the same way?

   brush : teeth

   Ⓐ toothbrush : dentist

   Ⓑ patient : receptionist

   Ⓒ wash : face

   Ⓓ office : restroom

4. Hana will sign in

   Ⓐ at the receptionist desk

   Ⓑ by the front door

   Ⓒ at the dental office

   Ⓓ in the children's room

5. Hana could see the dentist

   Ⓐ on Monday at 8:00

   Ⓑ on Saturday at 9:00

   Ⓒ on Thursday at 6:00

   Ⓓ on Tuesday at 2:00

Lian's New Color Book

These are new words to practice.

Say each word 10 times.

✳ start   ✳ picture

✳ connect   ✳ aunt

✳ animal   ✳ directions

✳ color   ✳ crayons

Choose one new word to write.

_____

- -

_____

Lian's New Color Book

Begin at "Start." Use your pencil. Draw a line to connect the dots. What animal do you see? Color the picture.

Lian's aunt came to see her. She gave Lian a color book. The book has animal pictures.

Lian turned to this page. She has not seen a page like this.

She read the directions. The words told her what to do. She got out her crayons.

Lian likes to color. She said "Thank you" to her aunt.

Lian's New Color Book

Look at the picture on page 28. Read the story.

Use the picture and the story to answer the questions.

1. To do this page, Lian will need

   Ⓐ glue

   Ⓑ scissors

   Ⓒ crayons

   Ⓓ ruler

2. The main idea of this story is

   Ⓐ to connect the dots

   Ⓑ to color an animal

   Ⓒ to read about an animal

   Ⓓ to help Lian

3. What will Lian do first?

   Ⓐ draw a line

   Ⓑ put her pencil on Start

   Ⓒ connect the dots

   Ⓓ color the picture

4. Think about how the word *draw* relates to the word *pencil*. Which words relate in the same way?

   draw : pencil

   Ⓐ glue : scissors

   Ⓑ start : finish

   Ⓒ animal : picture

   Ⓓ color : crayons

5. To *connect* the dots, Lian must

   Ⓐ draw a line from the first dot to the second dot

   Ⓑ cut out the dots and glue them together

   Ⓒ color the picture

   Ⓓ put tape on the page

Flowers

These are new words to practice.

Say each word 10 times.

✳ daisy   ✳ cut

✳ tulip   ✳ glue

✳ rose   ✳ carefully

✳ center   ✳ scissors

Choose one new word to write.

_____

- -

_____

Flowers

Color the daisy yellow. Color the tulip red. Color the rose in the center any color you like.

Color the leaves green. Cut out the leaves. Glue two leaves on each flower stem.

Ann's class read about flowers. Miss Kane gave each child this page. The class will color the page.

Ann read the directions carefully. She got out her crayons. She took out her scissors. Ann asked Miss Kane for the glue.

Ann colored the rose pink. She likes flowers.

Flowers

Look at the picture on page 31. Read the story.

Use the picture and the story to answer the questions.

1. The rose is

    Ⓐ first

    Ⓑ last

    Ⓒ in the center

    Ⓓ not on this page

2. This scene is mainly about

    Ⓐ coloring flowers

    Ⓑ tulips

    Ⓒ leaves

    Ⓓ growing plants

3. Think about how the word *rose* relates to the word *flower*. Which words relate in the same way?

rose : flower

    Ⓐ green : stem

    Ⓑ pine : tree

    Ⓒ cut : leaf

    Ⓓ pansy : cook

4. Ann should

    Ⓐ cut out the flowers

    Ⓑ color the leaves and glue them

    Ⓒ cut the leaves, then color

    Ⓓ color the leaves, then cut them out

5. A pansy is

    Ⓐ a small pan

    Ⓑ a flower

    Ⓒ a leaf

    Ⓓ a color

Reading Directions

These are new words to practice.

Say each word 10 times.

> ❋ copy ❋ finish
>
> ❋ write ❋ basket
>
> ❋ corner ❋ over
>
> ❋ back ❋ paper

Choose one new word to write.

_____

- - - - - - - - - - - - - - - - -

_____

Reading Directions

Copy these words. Write three sentences with these words. Write your name in the right corner.

sun rain clouds

Turn your paper over. On the back write three new words. When you finish, put your paper in the basket.

Steve came in the classroom. He saw these directions on the board. The words told the class what to do.

Mr. Green told the class to get a pencil. He gave paper to each person.

Steve put his name on his paper. He wrote the words he saw. He wrote sentences.

Steve wrote three new words. He wrote the words day, star, and wind. He put his paper in the basket.

34

Reading Directions

Look at the picture on page 34. Read the story.
Use the picture and the story to answer the questions.

1. This story is mainly about

    Ⓐ reading directions on the board

    Ⓑ getting a pencil

    Ⓒ turning the paper over

    Ⓓ coming into the classroom

2. In this story, Steve will

    Ⓐ color a picture

    Ⓑ practice writing

    Ⓒ copy words and write sentences

    Ⓓ get the answer from a friend

3. The directions say to

    Ⓐ read three sentences

    Ⓑ write three sentences

    Ⓒ get a pencil

    Ⓓ put your paper in your desk

4. In this story, *copy* means to

    Ⓐ take someone's idea

    Ⓑ ask the teacher

    Ⓒ make up your own words

    Ⓓ write the same words

5. Think about how the word *write* relates to the word *name*. Which words relate in the same way?

write : name

    Ⓐ read : word

    Ⓑ front : back

    Ⓒ copy : cat

    Ⓓ over : paper

Taking a Test

These are new words to practice.

Say each word 10 times.

* student   * test

* correct   * female

* age   * male

* grade   * answer

Choose one new word to write.

_____

- - - - - - - - - - - - - - - - - - - -

_____

Taking a Test

Write your name on the first line. Write your teacher's name on the second line.

Student's Name _____

Teacher's Name _____

Age   Grade   Fill in the correct circles to show your age and grade.

Write today's date. _____

Write your birth date. _____

Miss Gates gave each child a test book. She told the class to look at the back of the book. Juan saw a page like this.

Juan wrote his name. Then he wrote Miss Gates' name. Miss Gates said she would write the school name.

Juan colored a circle with a zero. He colored a circle with a six. Juan is six years old. He colored the circle with a one to show he is in first grade.

Miss Gates said she would read directions to the class. Juan will listen.

He will read sentences. He will mark the correct answer.

Taking a Test

Look at the picture on page 37. Read the story.

Use the picture and the story to answer the questions.

1. In what grade is Juan?

   Ⓐ second grade

   Ⓑ sixth grade

   Ⓒ zero grade

   Ⓓ first grade

2. This story is mainly about

   Ⓐ filling in a test book

   Ⓑ reading the test

   Ⓒ taking the test home

   Ⓓ coloring pictures

3. Why did Juan color the circle with a 1?

   Ⓐ Juan is in first grade.

   Ⓑ Juan is a boy.

   Ⓒ Juan writes numbers.

   Ⓓ Juan is in Miss Gates' class.

4. For each question, Juan will mark the *correct* answer. He will mark the space he thinks is

   Ⓐ a good answer

   Ⓑ the right answer

   Ⓒ the wrong answer

   Ⓓ his friend's choice

5. Think about how the word *mark* relates to the word *answer*. Which words relate in the same way?

   mark : answer

   Ⓐ student : teacher

   Ⓑ child : six

   Ⓒ read : sentence

   Ⓓ girl : boy

Making a Caterpillar

These are new words to practice.

Say each word 10 times.

✳ solid   ✳ place

✳ line   ✳ draw

✳ listen   ✳ follow

✳ fold   ✳ dotted

Choose one new word to write.

_____

- -

_____

Making a Caterpillar

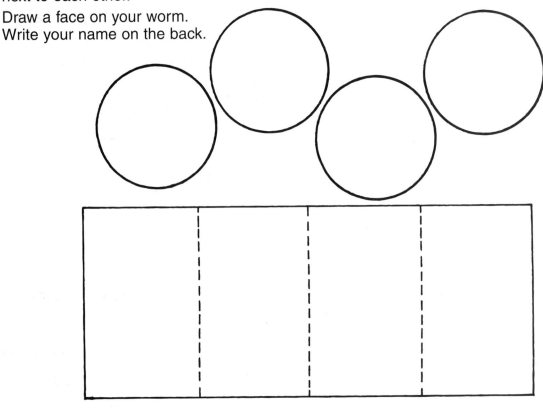

Cut on the solid lines. Color the circles green. Cut out the circles.

Listen to directions. Your teacher will tell you how to fold your paper.

Place one circle by each fold line. The circles will form a long worm. Glue the circles next to each other.

Draw a face on your worm.
Write your name on the back.

Kate heard a story about a long worm. Now she will make one from paper.

Kate will read directions. She will listen to her teacher.

Kate reads her paper. She listens to her teacher. She follows directions.

Miss Hamm says, "Fold the long strip on the first dotted line. Turn your paper over.

Fold on the next dotted line. Turn your paper over.

Fold on the next dotted line. Do this for each dotted line."

Kate colors her long worm green. She draws a funny face. She names her worm "Chris."

Making a Caterpillar

Look at the picture on page 40. Read the story.

Use the picture and the story to answer the questions.

1. Where should Kate write her name?

   (A) on the circles

   (B) on the front

   (C) on the dotted line

   (D) on the back

2. This story is mainly about

   (A) folding paper

   (B) making a caterpillar

   (C) reading a story

   (D) drawing circles

3. Kate will *fold* the paper. She will

   (A) tear the paper in half

   (B) cut the paper

   (C) bring the edges of the paper together

   (D) turn the paper over

4. Think about how the word *read* relates to the word *directions*. Which words relate in the same way?

read : directions

   (A) listen : teacher

   (B) draw : write

   (C) glue : paste

   (D) cut : circles

5. Which statement is not on the paper?

   (A) write your name on the back

   (B) cut on the dotted lines

   (C) color the circles green

   (D) draw a face on the caterpillar

The Pumpkin Patch

These are new words to practice.

Say each word 10 times.

✶ bring	✶ permission
✶ pumpkin	✶ slip
✶ patch	✶ sign
✶ field trip	✶ boots

Choose one new word to write.

_____

- -

_____

The Pumpkin Patch

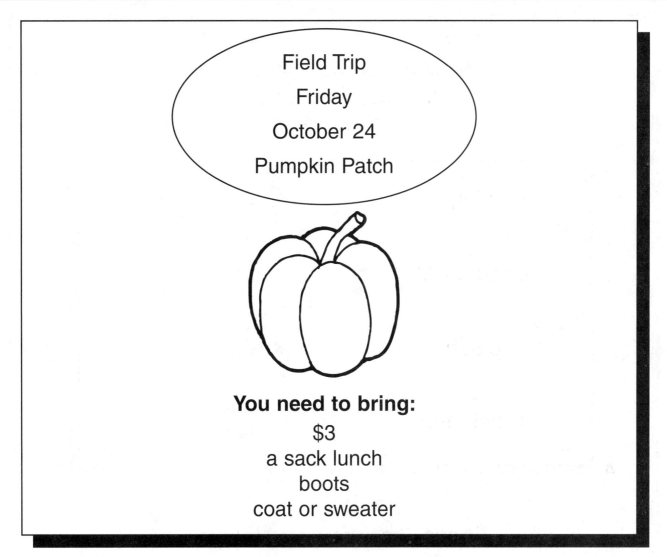

Field Trip

Friday

October 24

Pumpkin Patch

You need to bring:
$3
a sack lunch
boots
coat or sweater

Luke's class is going on a field trip. They will go to the pumpkin patch.

Mr. Cole gave each child this page. It tells about the field trip. He also gave them each a permission slip.

Luke took the permission slip home. He asked his mom to sign it.

He asked if he could have an apple for lunch. He also asked for a juice box.

It is the day of the field trip. Luke wore his boots to school. He brought his lunch. He brought a coat. Luke is ready for the field trip.

The Pumpkin Patch

Look at the picture on page 43. Read the story.

Use the picture and the story to answer the questions.

1. Luke's mom signed the *permission slip*. This means

   Ⓐ he can go outside

   Ⓑ he can go on the field trip

   Ⓒ he has a paper

   Ⓓ his mom will go on the field trip

2. This story is mainly about

   Ⓐ picking a pumpkin

   Ⓑ getting permission

   Ⓒ going on a field trip

   Ⓓ packing a lunch

3. Think about how the word *pumpkin* relates to the word *patch*. Which words relate in the same way?

   > **pumpkin : patch**

   Ⓐ juice box : lunch

   Ⓑ boots : school

   Ⓒ coat : sweater

   Ⓓ field : trip

4. How much money should Luke bring?

   Ⓐ $3

   Ⓑ $2

   Ⓒ $5

   Ⓓ $2

5. Luke will bring a sack lunch because

   Ⓐ he lost his lunch box

   Ⓑ he can throw it away after he eats

   Ⓒ he can keep the sack

   Ⓓ it will fit in the class lunch basket

Helping in the Kitchen

These are new words to practice.
Say each word 10 times.

❋ dish soap   ❋ counter

❋ kitchen   ❋ cheese

❋ hand soap   ❋ stove

❋ towel   ❋ sandwich

Choose one new word to write.

_____

- -

_____

Helping in the Kitchen

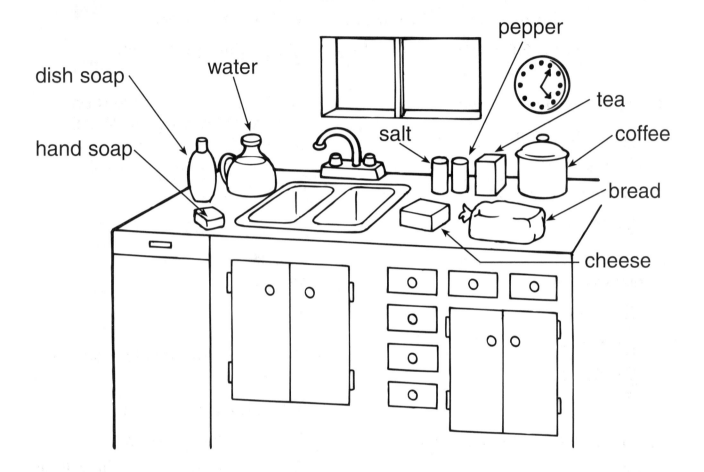

Sue wants to help in the kitchen. She and her mom will cook. Her mom tells her to wash her hands.

Sue washes her hands. She uses hand soap. She uses hot water. She dries her hands on a towel.

Sue's mom asks her to get the bread. It is on the counter. Sue gives her mom the bread. She hands her mom the cheese.

Sue's mom cuts a slice of cheese. She puts it on the bread.

She turns on the stove. She puts the bread and cheese in a pan. She turns off the stove.

Sue eats the sandwich. She helps wash dishes. Sue's mom says, "Thank you for your help."

Helping in the Kitchen

Look at the picture on page 46. Read the story.

Use the picture and the story to answer the questions.

1. This story is mainly about

    Ⓐ helping in the kitchen

    Ⓑ cleaning

    Ⓒ salt and pepper

    Ⓓ cooking

2. What did Sue use to wash dishes?

    Ⓐ hand soap

    Ⓑ coffee

    Ⓒ dish soap

    Ⓓ tea

3. Sue washed her hands with

    Ⓐ salt

    Ⓑ hand soap

    Ⓒ water

    Ⓓ a towel

4. Think about how the word *on* relates to the word *off*. Which words relate in the same way?

on : off

    Ⓐ soap : water

    Ⓑ bread : cheese

    Ⓒ coffee : tea

    Ⓓ hot : cold

5. Why did Sue's mom turn on the stove?

    Ⓐ to heat the kitchen

    Ⓑ to cook a sandwich

    Ⓒ to show Sue how to turn it on

    Ⓓ to make a fire

Circus Crunch

These are new words to practice.
Say each word 10 times.

✳ serving	✳ sticker
✳ breakfast	✳ item
✳ cereal	✳ grain
✳ prize	✳ vitamins

Choose one new word to write.

_____

- - - - - - - - - - - - - - - - - -

_____

Circus Crunch

Liz is eating breakfast. She wants to have cereal.

She sets the cereal on the table. She gets out the milk. Liz gets a bowl and a spoon.

Liz eats the cereal. She reads the box. It has a prize in it.

Liz looks in the box. She finds shiny stickers.

The box lists the items in the cereal. It has grain and sugar. It has vitamins in it.

Liz reads about a bigger prize. She can send in three box tops. Liz can get a watch.

Her mom says she may save box tops. Liz is glad. She likes Circus Crunch.

Circus Crunch

Look at the picture on page 49. Read the story.

Use the picture and the story to answer the questions.

1. What *prize* is in this box of cereal?

   Ⓐ a spoon

   Ⓑ a watch

   Ⓒ money

   Ⓓ stickers

2. This story is mainly about

   Ⓐ breakfast

   Ⓑ a box of cereal

   Ⓒ a watch

   Ⓓ stickers

3. This cereal most likely has

   Ⓐ animal shapes

   Ⓑ letter shapes

   Ⓒ bright colors

   Ⓓ candy pieces

4. You get it from food. You need it for good health.

   Ⓐ sugar

   Ⓑ milk

   Ⓒ vitamins

   Ⓓ grain

5. Think about how the word *breakfast* relates to the word *cereal*. Which words relate in the same way?

   breakfast : cereal

   Ⓐ spoon : bowl

   Ⓑ lunch : sandwich

   Ⓒ prize : sticker

   Ⓓ animals : circus

Tim Takes Care of His Puppy

These are new words to practice.
Say each word 10 times.

* flea   * fetch

* pet   * chew

* walk   * collar

* brush   * leash

Choose one new word to write.

Tim Takes Care of His Puppy

Tim has a new pet. He has to take care of his puppy. Each day Tim checks his job chart.

He takes the puppy for a walk. He gives it food and water. Tim brushes his puppy.

Tim plays with his puppy. He throws a stick. "Fetch!" The puppy gets the stick.

The puppy has a bone to chew. It has a collar and a leash. The puppy has a bed. Tim takes good care of his puppy.

Tim Takes Care of His Puppy

Look at the picture on page 52. Read the story.

Use the picture and the story to answer the questions.

1. A small bug that lives on animals is

   Ⓐ a flea

   Ⓑ an ant

   Ⓒ a bee

   Ⓓ a worm

2. This story is mainly about

   Ⓐ Tim's jobs

   Ⓑ playing with a puppy

   Ⓒ getting a pet

   Ⓓ taking care of a puppy

3. Think about how the word *puppy* relates to the word *dog*. Which words relate in the same way?

   puppy : dog

   Ⓐ food : water

   Ⓑ walk : leash

   Ⓒ boy : man

   Ⓓ collar : brush

4. How many jobs does Tim do to take care of his puppy?

   Ⓐ three

   Ⓑ four

   Ⓒ one

   Ⓓ two

5. Tim puts puppy bites in the food dish. In the other dish he most likely puts

   Ⓐ water

   Ⓑ bread

   Ⓒ food

   Ⓓ bones

Recycle Day

These are new words to practice.

Say each word 10 times.

✳ garbage   ✳ bin

✳ recycle   ✳ sort

✳ newspaper   ✳ glass

✳ paper   ✳ plastic

Choose one new word to write.

_____

- -

_____

Recycle Day

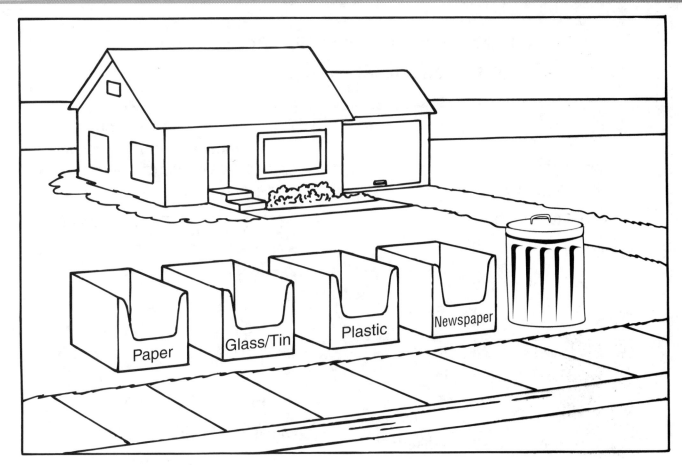

Today is garbage day. Ken helps his dad.

Ken takes items out to recycle. His dad takes the garbage out.

Ken's mom washes cans. Ken puts newspapers in a pile. He gets old mail and papers. Ken takes things to the recycle bins.

Ken sorts paper. He sorts glass and plastic. A milk jug goes in the plastic bin. He puts a jar in the glass bin.

Ken's dad is glad to have help. It is good to recycle.

Recycle Day

Look at the picture on page 55. Read the story.

Use the picture and the story to answer the questions.

1. This story is mainly about

   Ⓐ garbage day

   Ⓑ Ken's family

   Ⓒ how to recycle

   Ⓓ paper

2. The bin for glass is

   Ⓐ on the left

   Ⓑ on the right

   Ⓒ next to the paper bin

   Ⓓ in the center

3. The big gray can is most likely for

   Ⓐ bags

   Ⓑ cans

   Ⓒ garbage

   Ⓓ water

4. Think about how the word *newspaper* relates to the word *paper*. Which words relate in the same way?

newspaper : paper

   Ⓐ gray : plastic

   Ⓑ garbage : trash

   Ⓒ recycle : sort

   Ⓓ can : tin

5. When you *recycle*, you

   Ⓐ turn it around

   Ⓑ you use something old to make something new

   Ⓒ ride your bike

   Ⓓ throw it away

Packing for a Trip

These are new words to practice.

Say each word 10 times.

✳ toothpaste	✳ shampoo
✳ kit	✳ trip
✳ lotion	✳ pack
✳ soap	✳ comb

Choose one new word to write.

Packing for a Trip

Jeff's family is going on a trip. He must pack a bag. He walks to the bathroom.

Jeff's mom set things out. He will need his toothbrush. He needs toothpaste.

Jeff puts a comb in the bag. He packs soap. He packs shampoo.

Jeff tells his mom he is done. She comes to check. He is not done!

His mom adds the sun lotion to the bag. She puts in Jeff's bee sting kit. Now Jeff is ready for the trip.

Packing for a Trip

Look at the picture on page 58. Read the story.

Use the picture and the story to answer the questions.

1. Jeff is taking a *trip*. He will

   Ⓐ make a mistake

   Ⓑ fall down

   Ⓒ go somewhere

   Ⓓ write something

2. Jeff's bag is

   Ⓐ by the sink

   Ⓑ in the drawer

   Ⓒ under the sink

   Ⓓ by the soap

3. This story is mainly about

   Ⓐ what Jeff will do on a trip

   Ⓑ what Jeff will take on a trip

   Ⓒ where Jeff is going on a trip

   Ⓓ where Jeff keeps things

4. Think about how the word *soap* relates to the word *shampoo*. Which words relate in the same way?

   soap : shampoo

   Ⓐ sun : lotion

   Ⓑ comb : brush

   Ⓒ bee : sting

   Ⓓ pack : trip

5. Why does Jeff need shampoo?

   Ⓐ to color a bath tub

   Ⓑ to wash the dog

   Ⓒ to comb his hair

   Ⓓ to wash his hair

The Lemonade Stand

These are new words to practice.

Say each word 10 times.

* ice   * squeeze

* lemonade   * lemon

* recipe   * sugar

* pitcher   * sell

Choose one new word to write.

_____

- -

_____

The Lemonade Stand

Lemonade

3 lemons
6 tablespoons sugar
3 cups water
ice cubes

Squeeze juice out of lemons.

Add water.

Mix in sugar. Stir well. Pour over ice cubes.

It is hot outside. Erin wants to make lemonade. She asks her mom. Her mom says she can.

Erin's mom sets out the recipe. Erin gets a pitcher. She gets other things she will need.

Erin reads the recipe. She squeezes lemons. She adds water and sugar.

She has some to drink. It tastes good.

Erin wants to sell the lemonade. She asks her mom. Erin's friends will like lemonade on this hot day.

The Lemonade Stand

**Read the recipe on page 61. Read the story.
Use the recipe and the story to answer the questions.**

1. This story is mainly about

    (A) a hot day

    (B) Erin's friends

    (C) lemonade

    (D) Erin's mom

2. After Erin puts in the sugar she will

    (A) stir it all together

    (B) squeeze the lemons

    (C) add water

    (D) put in ice cubes

3. Why did Erin put sugar in the lemonade?

    (A) sugar tastes sour

    (B) her mom said she should

    (C) lemons are sour

    (D) ice cubes will melt

4. Think about how the word *lemons* relates to the word *juice.* Which words relate in the same way?

    lemon : juice

    (A) make : sell

    (B) pitcher : water

    (C) sugar : stir

    (D) ice : cubes

5. When you *squeeze* a *lemon*, you

    (A) put it in a small space

    (B) press the sides together

    (C) step on it

    (D) cut it apart

Saturday Cleaning

These are new words to practice.

Say each word 10 times.

* window

* dresser

* bookcase

* shake

* closet

* broom

* clothes

* sweep

Choose one new word to write.

Saturday Cleaning

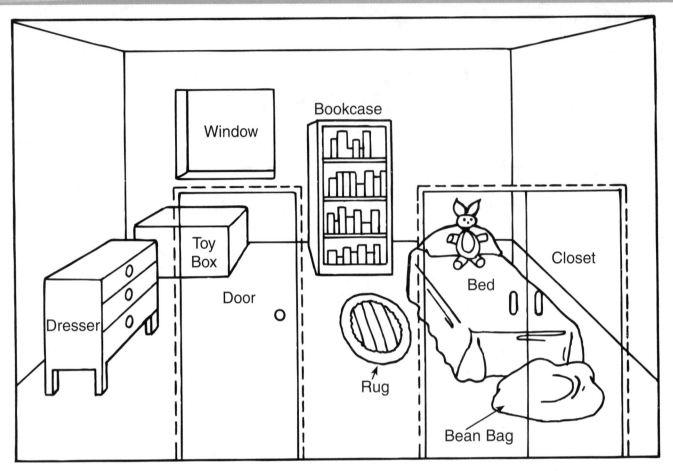

Today is Saturday. Rafe will clean his room. Then he may go out to play.

First Rafe picks up his toys. He puts the books away. He puts his clothes in the dresser.

Rafe must make his bed. He puts his teddy bear on the bed. He shakes out the rug.

Rafe gets the broom. He sweeps the floor. Rafe's room is clean. He is ready to play.

Saturday Cleaning

Look at the picture on page 64. Read the story.

Use the picture and the story to answer the questions.

1. Where did Rafe put his clothes?

   (A) on the bed

   (B) in the dresser

   (C) on the bookcase

   (D) in the closet

2. Rafe *shakes* the rug. He

   (A) takes it apart

   (B) upsets it

   (C) grabs its hand

   (D) moves it quickly up and down

3. This story is mainly about

   (A) cleaning a room

   (B) playing outside

   (C) putting away clothes

   (D) shaking the rug

4. Think about how the word *make* relates to the word *bed*. Which words relate in the same way?

make : bed

   (A) dresser : toy box

   (B) toys : books

   (C) sweep : floor

   (D) window : closet

5. Where did Rafe put his toys?

   (A) the closet

   (B) the toy box

   (C) the bookcase

   (D) under the bed

June Fun

These are new words to practice.
Say each word 10 times.

✳ band	✳ club
✳ concert	✳ practice
✳ calendar	✳ team
✳ events	✳ busy

Choose one new word to write.

_____

- -

_____

June Fun

June

Sunday	Monday	Tuesday	Wednesday	Thursday	Friday	Saturday
				1 Kid's Club	**2**	**3** Picnic
4	**5** Baseball	**6**	**7**	**8** Kid's Club	**9** Zoo Trip	**10** Ball Game
11	**12** Baseball	**13** Band Concert	**14**	**15** Kid's Club	**16** Last Day of School	**17**
18	**19** Baseball	**20**	**21**	**22** Kid's Club	**23**	**24**
25	**26** Baseball	**27**	**28**	**29** Kid's Club	**30**	

A calendar shows what day it is. Lynn's mom has a calendar. She writes events on it.

Lynn's class is going to the zoo. They will go on June 9. Lynn's mom writes it down.

Lynn goes to Kids Club every Thursday.

Her brother Rob has baseball practice. It is on Mondays. His team will play a game on June 10.

The family will go on a picnic on June 3. They will have fun with friends. June is a busy month!

June Fun

Look at the calendar page on page 67. Read the story.

Use the calendar and the story to answer the questions.

1. This story is mainly about

   Ⓐ Lynn's class zoo trip

   Ⓑ Lynn's June calendar

   Ⓒ Lynn's family picnic

   Ⓓ Lynn's brother Rob

2. An *event* is

   Ⓐ the same number of something

   Ⓑ a problem

   Ⓒ something interesting or important that happens

   Ⓓ when someone asks you to go somewhere

3. What day of the week will Lynn go to the zoo?

   Ⓐ Saturday

   Ⓑ Tuesday

   Ⓒ Thursday

   Ⓓ Friday

4. Which of these is true?

   Ⓐ The last day of school is June 16.

   Ⓑ The last day of school is on a Saturday.

   Ⓒ The last day of school is June 9.

   Ⓓ The last day of school is in July.

5. Think about how the word *Wednesday* relates to the word *Thursday*. Which words relate in the same way?

   | **Wednesday : Thursday** |

   Ⓐ band : concert

   Ⓑ club : zoo

   Ⓒ Sunday : Monday

   Ⓓ team : game

Come to the Party

These are new words to practice.
Say each word 10 times.

✳ invitation	✳ present
✳ party	✳ blow
✳ yesterday	✳ candles
✳ bought	✳ balloon

Choose one new word to write.

_____

- - - - - - - - - - - - - - - - - -

_____

Come to the Party

Please Come

When: Sunday, March 26

Where: 211 Oak St.

Time: 1–3 P.M.

Who: for Greg

It's a Party!

Greg gave Ian a card. It was an invitation. Greg is having a birthday party.

Greg and Ian are friends. Yesterday Ian bought Greg a present. He got Greg a toy boat.

The party is at Greg's house. It will be in the afternoon.

Greg and his friends will play games.

They will eat cake. They will have ice cream.

Greg will blow out candles on the cake.

Ian hopes there will be balloons. He likes to pop balloons.

Come to the Party

Look at the picture on page 70. Read the story.

Use the picture and the story to answer the questions.

1. When did Ian buy Greg's present?

    (A) yesterday

    (B) Friday

    (C) Sunday

    (D) today

2. This story is mainly about

    (A) a present

    (B) a toy boat

    (C) a party

    (D) a friend

3. Think about how the word *pop* relates to the word *balloons*. Which words relate in the same way?

    pop : balloons

    (A) games : party

    (B) blow : candles

    (C) present : birthday

    (D) cake : ice cream

4. From the picture on the card, you can tell this is for a

    (A) Christmas party

    (B) birthday party

    (C) Fourth of July party

    (D) picnic

5. When someone gives you an *invitation*, they

    (A) ask you to talk

    (B) give you cake and ice cream

    (C) make something for you

    (D) ask you to go somewhere

Maki's Day at School

These are new words to practice.
Say each word 10 times.

* recess   * social studies

* journal   * library

* silent   * schedule

* aloud   * daily

Choose one new word to write.

_____

- - - - - - - - - - - - - - - - -

_____

Maki's Day at School

8:30	Flag salute Circle time
9:00	Math Snack
10:00	Recess
10:15	Reading Spelling Journal writing Silent reading
11:30	Lunch
12:00	Read aloud
12:15	Social studies or science
1:00	Writing
1:30	Recess
1:45	Activity
2:15	Centers
2:45	Clean up
3:00	Go home

<u>Activity 1:45</u>

Monday—P. E.
Tuesday—Library
Wednesday—P. E.
Thursday—Music
Friday—Art

Maki walked in the classroom. She saw a new class schedule on the board. Mrs. Will changed the daily times.

Before, Maki's class had math after lunch. Now math is in the morning.

Maki likes writing best. Spelling is her worst subject.

Every day Maki does many of the same things. Each day has new things, too. Maki likes school.

Maki's Day at School

Look at the schedule on page 73. Read the story.

Use the schedule and the story to answer the questions.

1. A *schedule* shows

   Ⓐ what day comes next

   Ⓑ what time things happen

   Ⓒ how to do math

   Ⓓ what Mrs. Will teaches

2. This story is mainly about

   Ⓐ Maki's daily class schedule

   Ⓑ what time Maki does things

   Ⓒ what day Maki has P.E.

   Ⓓ what Maki likes to do

3. What comes after math?

   Ⓐ recess

   Ⓑ reading

   Ⓒ writing

   Ⓓ snack

4. Think about how the word *before* relates to the word *after*. Which words relate in the same way?

before : after

   Ⓐ same : new

   Ⓑ silent : reading

   Ⓒ best : worst

   Ⓓ spelling : writing

5. What day does Maki's class go to music?

   Ⓐ Tuesday

   Ⓑ Thursday

   Ⓒ Monday

   Ⓓ Wednesday

Day Camp

These are new words to practice.
Say each word 10 times.

* camp   * explore

* craft   * choice

* nature   * peak

* quiet   * during

Choose one new word to write.

_____

- -

_____

GREEN HILLS DAY CAMP

Tuesday, June 23

9:00	Story Time
9:30	Craft
10:00	Nature Walk
10:30	Snack
11:00	Boat Races
12:00	Lunch
12:30	Quiet Time
1:00	Games
2:00	Free Time
3:00	Go Home

* Come to Craft Time! We will make bird feeders.

* Today's walk will explore the pond.

* Free Time Choices:
  Hike to Look Out Peak
  Craft—Kites
  Swim

It is summer. Rob goes to day camp. He reads the news board. It says what will happen today.

Rob wants to go on the nature walk. He will see fish at the pond. He might catch a bug.

Rob likes game time. He can run fast. He plays with his friends.

It is hot today. During free time Rob will swim. Today is a good day at camp.

Day Camp

Look at the schedule on page 76. Read the story.
Use the schedule and the story to answer the questions.

1. This story is mainly about
   - Ⓐ How to make a bird feeder
   - Ⓑ what to do at day camp
   - Ⓒ where to hike
   - Ⓓ who will race a boat

2. Rob will find out what the pond is like. He will
   - Ⓐ explore it
   - Ⓑ see it
   - Ⓒ think about it
   - Ⓓ look for it

3. Which statement is not true?
   - Ⓐ Rob will explore the pond.
   - Ⓑ Rob will swim.
   - Ⓒ Rob will make a kite.
   - Ⓓ Rob will hear a story.

4. Think about how the word *walk* relates to the word *hike*. Which words relate in the same way?

   | walk : hike |

   - Ⓐ snack : lunch
   - Ⓑ craft : kite
   - Ⓒ game : race
   - Ⓓ swim : hot

5. Right after snack, Rob can
   - Ⓐ play a game
   - Ⓑ explore the pond
   - Ⓒ make a bird feeder
   - Ⓓ race a boat

Ben's Chores

These are new words to practice.
Say each word 10 times.

✻ job	✻ help
✻ chart	✻ set
✻ morning	✻ chores
✻ afternoon	✻ able

Choose one new word to write.

_____

- - - - - - - - - - - - - - - - - -

_____

Ben's Chores

Morning	Sunday	Monday	Tuesday	Wednesday	Thursday	Friday	Saturday
Make bed		X	X				
Give water to dog	X	X	X				
Feed the dog	X	X	X				

Afternoon	Sunday	Monday	Tuesday	Wednesday	Thursday	Friday	Saturday
Pick up toys	X	X					
Set the table	X		X				
Help with dishes	X	X	X				

Ben has chores to do every day. He cleans his room. He helps his mom. He takes care of the dog.

Ben checks off a job when he does it. Today is Tuesday. Ben has not done all his chores.

Ben does some chores in the morning. Some jobs he does in the afternoon.

He sets the table for dinner. He helps put away dishes.

Friday night Ben is going to his friend's house. He will do his afternoon chores. He will not be able to do his chores on Saturday.

Ben's Chores

Look at the chart on page 79. Read the story.

Use the chart and the story to answer the questions.

1. Which chore has Ben not done today?

   (A) make his bed

   (B) pick up toys

   (C) help his mom

   (D) feed the dog

2. A *chore* is a job you do

   (A) when you want to

   (B) at your friend's house

   (C) every day

   (D) at work

3. This story is mainly about

   (A) Ben's visit with his friend

   (B) Ben's mom

   (C) Ben's dog

   (D) Ben's chores

4. Ben will be at his friend's house Saturday morning. Which job will he not be able to do?

   (A) give water to the dog

   (B) make his bed

   (C) set the table

   (D) pick up toys

5. Think about how the word *chore* relates to the word *job*. Which words relate in the same way?

chore : job

   (A) morning : afternoon

   (B) make : bed

   (C) set : clean

   (D) able : can

What Is on TV?

These are new words to practice.

Say each word 10 times.

* channel ✳ cartoon

✳ DVD ✳ remote control

✳ watch ✳ show

✳ movie ✳ favorite

Choose one new word to write.

_____

- - - - - - - - - - - - - - - - -

_____

What Is on TV?

Channel	5:00	5:30	6:00	6:30	7:00	7:30	8:00
2 CBA	News	News	News	News	Family Game Show	Family Game Show	Rose and Dan
6 NBS	News	News	News	News	Music Today	Dance on the Town	Crime Scenes
8 ANS	News	News	News	News	Homes on Parade	Homes on Parade	Cooking Light
10 SBP	Amazing Animals	Amazing Animals	Classic Cars	Money Today	Science Sam	Science Sam	Finding Rocks
12 BOX	American Court	American Court	The Marby House	Get Real	Get Real	Road Race	USA Stage
49 KDS	Genie Girls	Wolf Dog	City Beat	Todd's Life	Frantic Friday	Today's Tales	Backyard Day Care (movie)

Scott may watch two hours of TV during the week. Or, he may watch one DVD. He cannot watch any TV before school.

After school Scott does homework. He plays outside. He eats dinner.

Scott gets ready for bed. He reads a book.

On Friday Scott may watch a TV movie. He uses the remote control. He finds the channel. Saturday Scott may watch cartoons.

Scott likes animal shows. His favorite is *Wolf Dog*.

What Is on TV?

Look at the chart on page 82. Read the story.

Use the chart and the story to answer the questions.

1. Scott's favorite show is *Wolf Dog.* It is

   Ⓐ the show he likes best

   Ⓑ the show Scott's dad watches

   Ⓒ the show he does not watch

   Ⓓ the show that is after the news

2. This story is mainly about

   Ⓐ animal shows

   Ⓑ watching TV

   Ⓒ cartoons

   Ⓓ watching movies

3. Scott likes animal shows. What other animal show could he watch?

   Ⓐ *Today's Tales*

   Ⓑ *Cooking Light*

   Ⓒ *Amazing Animals*

   Ⓓ *Finding Rocks*

4. Think about how the word *may* relates to the word *cannot.* Which words relate in the same way?

may : cannot

   Ⓐ remote: control

   Ⓑ before: after

   Ⓒ game: show

   Ⓓ movie: DVD

5. When can Scott watch an animal show?

   Ⓐ 6:00 P.M.

   Ⓑ 7:00 P.M.

   Ⓒ 6:30 P.M.

   Ⓓ 5:00 P.M.

Guess My Game

These are new words to practice.
Say each word 10 times.

* play   * sport

* object   * point

* guess   * rules

* describe   * group

Choose one new word to write.

_____

- -

_____

Guess My Game

Players

6 to 10 people

Things You Need

- one piece of paper for each person
- pencils
- hat

Object

Guess the person who is described

How to Play

One person is "It." Give each person a paper. Write the sport you like best.

Fold your paper. Each person puts a paper in the hat.

"It" takes one paper out. Read the sport aloud.

Take turns guessing who wrote that sport. The person who guesses right gets one point.

Joan's class will play a game. Each group has eight people. Mr. Slane gives each group the rules to play.

Joan gets a piece of paper. It says *swim*. She likes to swim. Joan writes "swim" on her paper. She puts it in the hat.

Paul is "It." He takes a paper out. He reads the paper. It says *running*.

It is Joan's turn to guess. She thinks Todd wrote the paper.

Joan is right. She gets one point.

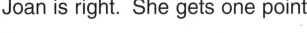

Guess My Game

Read the game directions on page 85. Read the story.

Use the game directions and the story to answer the questions.

1. This story is mainly about

    (A) putting paper in a hat

    (B) showing a sport

    (C) guessing who likes a sport

    (D) being "It"

2. Each player writes

    (A) a sport

    (B) a name

    (C) a food

    (D) a color

3. Think about how the word *guess* relates to the word *sport*. Which words relate in the same way?

guess : sport

    (A) pencil : hat

    (B) it : player

    (C) write : pencil

    (D) play : game

4. The *object* of a game is

    (A) what you see

    (B) what you play with

    (C) what you are trying to do

    (D) who wins

5. After Joan folds her paper, she will

    (A) write on it

    (B) put it in the hat

    (C) take it out of the hat

    (D) get a point

People, Places, and Things

These are new words to practice.
Say each word 10 times.

✳ card	✳ turn
✳ noun	✳ win
✳ stack	✳ deck
✳ clue	✳ printed

Choose one new word to write.

_____

- - - - - - - - - - - - - - - - - - - -

_____

People, Places, and Things

Players

3 to 6 people

Things You Need

5 noun cards for each player

Object

Guess the most cards correctly

How to Play

Stack the cards so the words do not show. The first player takes one card. Give clues to describe the word. Do not say the word that is on the card.

The other players guess the word. Each person gets one guess.

The person who guesses correctly gets the card. That person takes the next card. The person with the most cards wins.

Trent has a new card game. The game has a deck of cards. Each card has a noun printed on it.

Trent will play with Ray and Hans. Ray takes the first turn. His card says *tree*.

Ray tells Trent and Hans the noun is big and green. Trent guesses a house. Hans guesses a tree.

Hans gets the card. Now it is his turn.

People, Places, and Things

Read the game directions on page 88. Read the story.

Use the game directions and the story to answer the questions.

1. How many cards do you use?

    (A) all of them

    (B) five for each person

    (C) four for each person

    (D) one deck

2. Each card has a *noun*. The word could be

    (A) a color

    (B) something new

    (C) an action

    (D) a person, place, or thing

3. This game is mainly about

    (A) guessing words

    (B) stacking cards

    (C) playing with friends

    (D) taking cards

4. Ray takes the first turn. He will

    (A) stack the cards

    (B) guess a noun

    (C) keep the card

    (D) take a card

5. Think about how the word *stack* relates to the word *cards*. Which words relate in the same way?

    | stack : cards |

    (A) player : printed

    (B) noun : clue

    (C) describe : word

    (D) guess : win

Summer Camp

These are new words to practice.

Say each word 10 times.

* insert   * screen

* disk   * computer

* cursor   * icon

* click   * order

Choose one new word to write.

_____

- -

_____

Summer Camp

Setup

1. Insert the disk.
2. Move the cursor to the circle.
3. Click the mouse button to start the game.

Tam and his friends want to set up their camp. They want to cook food on the fire.

They want to set up their tent. It is getting dark. Tam wants to put the food where no animals can get it. He also wants to put the fire out.

What should Tam do if he is very hungry? He needs to store the food after he cooks it. He also wants to put the fire out soon.

Click the four icons in the right order.

Choose which task to do first. Click on that object.

Paul likes to play computer games. He wants to play this game. He puts the disk in the computer.

Paul clicks the play button. He sees the story screen. He reads the story.

Paul goes to the next screen. It shows the game.

Paul plays two times. He wins one game.

Summer Camp

Read the game directions on page 91. Read the story.

Use the game directions and the story to answer the questions.

1. What happens when you *click* a mouse?

   Ⓐ You tell the computer to do something.

   Ⓑ You push a button.

   Ⓒ You pull its tail.

   Ⓓ You tap it on the table.

2. Paul should click the

   Ⓐ food bag, then the pail

   Ⓑ food bag, then the fire

   Ⓒ fire, then the pail

   Ⓓ tent, then the fire

3. This game is mainly about

   Ⓐ eating

   Ⓑ camping

   Ⓒ cooking

   Ⓓ sleeping

4. Think about how the word *click* relates to the word *mouse*. Which words relate in the same way?

   click : mouse

   Ⓐ out : in

   Ⓑ computer : game

   Ⓒ camp : fire

   Ⓓ cook : food

5. Paul starts to play the game. He

   Ⓐ reads the story

   Ⓑ hears the story

   Ⓒ touches the story

   Ⓓ sees the story

Grandma's House

These are new words to practice.

Say each word 10 times.

✳ equipment	✳ treasure
✳ picture	✳ chip
✳ cube	✳ kitchen
✳ piece	✳ start

Choose one new word to write.

_____

- -

_____

Grandma's House

Players
2 to 4 people

Equipment
- game board
- picture cube
- one game piece for each player
- treasure chips
- grandma cards

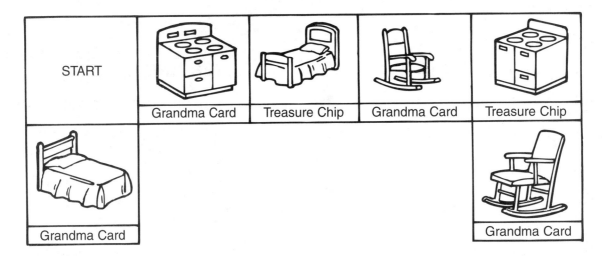

| START | Grandma Card | Treasure Chip | Grandma Card | Treasure Chip |

| Grandma Card | | | | Grandma Card |

Object
You need three grandma cards. You need two treasure chips. Then the game is over.

How to Play
Players place their game pieces on Start. The first player tosses the picture cube.
Move your game piece to the room the cube shows. Read the words in the room. Take a grandma card or get a treasure chip.

Ella is playing this game. She plays with Dee. They each put their pieces on start.

Dee tosses the cube. It shows the kitchen. Dee moves her piece to the kitchen.

She takes a grandma card. The card says *make cookies*. Dee keeps the card.

It is Ella's turn. Ella tosses the cube.

She moves to the bedroom. She gets a treasure. Now Ella has a treasure chip.

They keep playing. Soon Dee has three grandma cards. She has two treasure chips. Dee wins the game.

Grandma's House

Read the game directions on page 94. Read the story.

Use the game directions and the story to answer the questions.

1. Ella moved her piece to the bedroom. She

   Ⓐ made cookies

   Ⓑ got a treasure

   Ⓒ went to the rocker

   Ⓓ stayed in the bedroom

2. This game is mainly about

   Ⓐ doing things in Grandma's house

   Ⓑ making cookies

   Ⓒ getting treasure

   Ⓓ moving to rooms

3. Think about how the word *toss* relates to the word *cube*. Which words relate in the same way?

toss : cube

   Ⓐ kitchen : bedroom

   Ⓑ start : win

   Ⓒ move : piece

   Ⓓ rocker : teddy bear

4. Why did Dee win?

   Ⓐ she went back to start

   Ⓑ she had three Grandma cards and two treasure chips

   Ⓒ she got to the rocker first

   Ⓓ she made cookies with Grandma

5. The *equipment* is

   Ⓐ the picture cube

   Ⓑ what you use to make cookies

   Ⓒ a tool to build the house

   Ⓓ what you need to play the game

Kip and Kyle

These are new words to practice.

Say each word 10 times.

✳ control   ✳ defense

✳ warning   ✳ attack

✳ enemy   ✳ character

✳ protect   ✳ duck

Choose one new word to write.

_____

- -

_____

96

Kip and Kyle

Setup

1. Plug game box into TV.
2. Turn on TV and box.
3. Move control pad to choose game.
4. Press button to start a new game.

Object

Save the princess.

Characters

Kip

A jump

B duck—Kip's hair can protect him.

Kyle

A jump

B duck—Kyle's hair can be used to attack.

Snipe

Warning: Snipe can attack! He has no defense.
He attacks only if he sees you. His eye points one way.

Greber

Greber is an enemy. He has a strong helmet. He also has huge feet.

Playing the Game

Pick up objects by walking over them. Use the control pad. Move Kip or Kyle to the right.

Jump on Snipe to flatten him. Defend with Kip's hair. Attack with Kyle's hair.

Use Kyle to attack Greber.

Kip and Kyle are two brothers. They like to have fun at home.

Kip has long, shaggy hair. Kyle has hair with spikes.

Greber took the princess of the land. Kip and Kyle try to save her.

Kip's hair can block attacks. Kyle can attack with his hair.

They try to save the princess.

Kip and Kyle

Read the game directions on page 97. Read the story.

Use the game directions and the story to answer the questions.

1. Kip can *protect* himself when

   Ⓐ he runs

   Ⓑ he attacks

   Ⓒ he ducks

   Ⓓ he walks

2. This story is mainly about

   Ⓐ enemies

   Ⓑ Kip and Kyle

   Ⓒ a flag

   Ⓓ hair

3. Kyle *attacks* an *enemy* by

   Ⓐ sticking him with his hair

   Ⓑ jumping on him

   Ⓒ walking over him

   Ⓓ wearing a helmet

4. Think about how the word *protect* relates to the word *defend*. Which words relate in the same way?

   protect : defend

   Ⓐ warning : enemy

   Ⓑ start : begin

   Ⓒ attack : defense

   Ⓓ green : yellow

5. The object of the game is to

   Ⓐ save the princess

   Ⓑ protect yourself

   Ⓒ attack an enemy

   Ⓓ make Kip jump

Say, Do

These are new words to practice.

Say each word 10 times.

✳ ask	✳ choose
✳ team	✳ game
✳ task	✳ score
✳ turn	✳ tie

Choose one new word to write.

_____

- -

_____

Say, Do

Players

You need eight people. There are four people on each team.

Object

Ask the other team to do something they cannot do.

How to Play

The first team asks one person on the second team to do something. If the person cannot do it, the first team gets a point. The first team asks again.

If the person can do the task, it is the second team's turn. The second team asks the first team to do something.

Pat plays with her friends at recess. They choose to play a game. Pat's team goes first.

They ask Ty to hop on one foot. He must hop 10 times. Ty is on the second team. Ty cannot do it.

Pat's team gets a point. They get another turn. They ask Chris to stand on his head.

Chris can do it. It is the second team's turn.

Ty and Chris ask Pat to skip backward. She cannot do it. Ty's team gets a point.

The score is a tie. The bell rings. Recess is over.

Say, Do

Read the game directions on page 100. Read the story.

Use the game directions and the story to answer the questions.

1. This story is mainly about

    (A) getting points

    (B) asking questions

    (C) playing a game

    (D) skipping backward

2. What did Pat ask Chris to do?

    (A) play a game

    (B) jump ten times

    (C) skip backward

    (D) stand on his head

3. How many people are on a team in this game?

    (A) four people

    (B) eight people

    (C) a group of people

    (D) three people

4. A group of people who play a game are

    (A) friends

    (B) two people

    (C) a team

    (D) together

5. Think about how the word *hop* relates to the word *skip*. Which words relate in the same way?

    hop : skip

    (A) person : team

    (B) score : point

    (C) bell : recess

    (D) lose : win

Jean Goes to the Park

These are new words to practice.

Say each word 10 times.

✳ stay   ✳ area

✳ picnic   ✳ garden

✳ path   ✳ playground

✳ split   ✳ please

Choose one new word to write.

_____

- -

_____

      102

Jean Goes to the Park

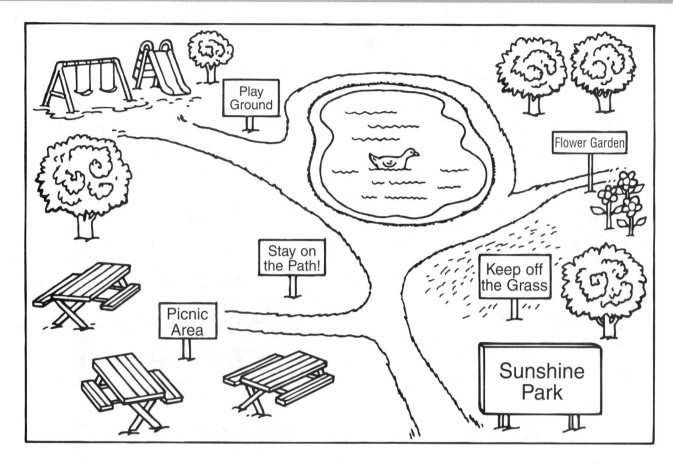

Jean likes to go to the park. She goes with her family. They bring a picnic.

Jean walks on the path. The path splits. Jean stays on the path to the right. She walks around the pond.

Her mother calls her. Jean runs to the picnic area. It is left of the pond. It is time to eat.

Jean Goes to the Park

Look at the picture on page 103. Read the story.
Use the picture and the story to answer the questions.

1. This story is mainly about

   Ⓐ a picnic

   Ⓑ a pond

   Ⓒ a park

   Ⓓ a path

2. The *picnic area* is

   Ⓐ to the left of the pond

   Ⓑ to the right of the pond

   Ⓒ by the flower garden

   Ⓓ to the right of the path

3. Jean goes to the park. It is a place

   Ⓐ to plant flowers

   Ⓑ with trees and a playground

   Ⓒ with cars

   Ⓓ to stay

4. Where will Jean find the ducks?

   Ⓐ in the flower garden

   Ⓑ by the swings

   Ⓒ in the pond

   Ⓓ in the picnic area

5. Think about how the word *left* relates to the word *right*. Which words relate in the same way?

left : right

   Ⓐ on : off

   Ⓑ picnic : play

   Ⓒ grass : flowers

   Ⓓ park : path

Fire Safety Plan

These are new words to practice.
Say each word 10 times.

✻ door	✻ route
✻ window	✻ arrow
✻ safety	✻ escape
✻ plan	✻ danger

Choose one new word to write.

Fire Safety Plan

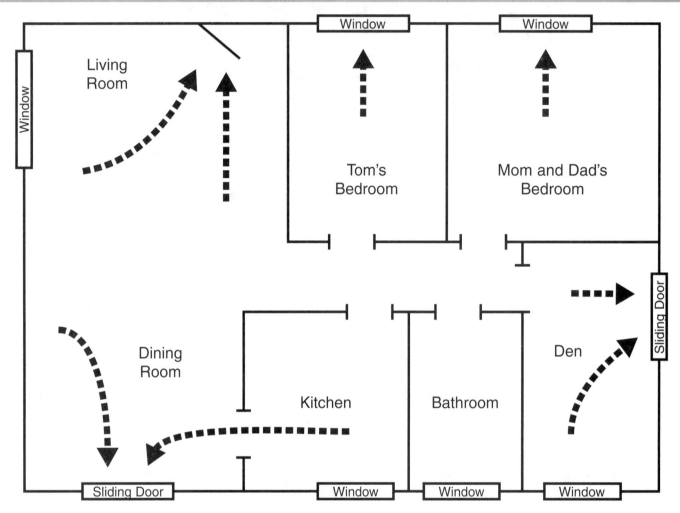

This week is Fire Safety Week. Tom has to make a fire safety plan. His dad helps him.

Tom makes a picture of his house. His dad helps him draw doors and windows. They plan a route to get out.

They put arrows in the picture. The arrows show how to get out.

Tom's family can escape from a fire. They will be safe from danger.

Fire Safety Plan

Look at the picture on page 106. Read the story.

Use the picture and the story to answer the questions.

1. When you *escape* from a fire, you
   - Ⓐ get out of danger
   - Ⓑ get away from someone
   - Ⓒ run in circles
   - Ⓓ call for help

2. This story is mainly about
   - Ⓐ how to open a door
   - Ⓑ how to find Tom's room
   - Ⓒ how to have a fire
   - Ⓓ how to get out if there is a fire

3. Think about how the word *door* relates to the word *window*. Which words relate in the same way?

   > **door : window**

   - Ⓐ safety: danger
   - Ⓑ arrows: escape
   - Ⓒ path: route
   - Ⓓ bedroom: bathroom

4. Which statement is not true:
   - Ⓐ It is easy to escape from Tom's house.
   - Ⓑ Every room has a door or a window.
   - Ⓒ Tom can get out the bathroom window.
   - Ⓓ Tom made a fire safety plan.

5. Why are there arrows in the picture?
   - Ⓐ to point to doors and windows
   - Ⓑ to show which way to go
   - Ⓒ to show the fire
   - Ⓓ to point to Tom's room

Kay's New School

These are new words to practice.
Say each word 10 times.

✻ computer	✻ new
✻ gym	✻ classroom
✻ library	✻ map
✻ office	✻ across

Choose one new word to write.

_____

- - - - - - - - - - - - - - - - -

_____

Kay's New School

| Computer Room | | Grade 5 | Grade 5 | Music | Grade 4 | Grade 4 |

| Gym/ Lunch Room | | Grade 1 **X** | Library | | Grade 2 | Grade 3 |

| Kitchen | | Office | K | Grade 1 | Grade 2 | Grade 3 |

Kay's family just moved to a new town. Kay will go to a new school. She does not know how to find her classroom.

Her teacher gives Kay a map. It shows everything in the school. The teacher writes a red X to show Kay her classroom.

The map helps Kay find places. She sees the lunch room is across from the kitchen.

She reads the map. The school does not seem so strange now.

Kay's New School

Look at the picture on page 109. Read the story.

Use the picture and the story to answer the questions.

1. Kay's classroom is next to

   (A) the third grade class

   (B) the music room

   (C) the kitchen

   (D) the library

2. This story is mainly about

   (A) how to get to school

   (B) how to find places at school

   (C) how to eat lunch

   (D) how to go to the library

3. How will Kay find the office?

   (A) walk across the hall

   (B) walk down the hall

   (C) walk to the gym

   (D) walk out the door

4. Where will Kay's class go to exercise?

   (A) the music room

   (B) the computer room

   (C) the gym

   (D) outside

5. Think about how the word *library* relates to the word *gym*. Which words relate in the same way?

   library : gym

   (A) classroom : desk

   (B) office : kitchen

   (C) across : down

   (D) school : book

Around the Zoo

These are new words to practice.
Say each word 10 times.

* seal   * giraffe

* hope   * find

* enjoy   * next

* Africa   * again

Choose one new word to write.

_____

- - - - - - - - - - - - - - - - - - -

_____

Around the Zoo

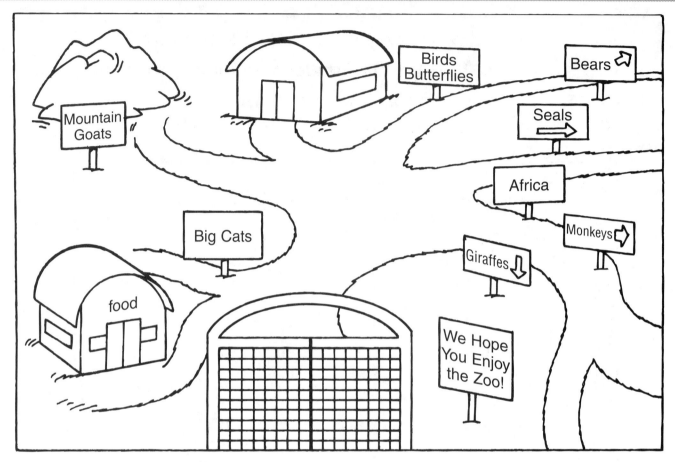

Jenn goes to the zoo. She gets a map at the gate. The map tells how to find animals.

Jenn wants to see the seals first. They are next to the bears. She goes to see the bears.

Jenn looks at the goats. Then she sees the big cats.

It is time to go. Jenn will not see the birds. She will come again.

Around the Zoo

Look at the picture on page 112. Read the story.
Use the picture and the story to answer the questions.

1. Which animals did Jenn see first?

   Ⓐ goats

   Ⓑ seals

   Ⓒ bears

   Ⓓ cats

2. This story is mainly about

   Ⓐ where to find each animal

   Ⓑ where to get food

   Ⓒ animals at the zoo

   Ⓓ how to get in the zoo

3. Think about how the word *bird* relates to the word *butterfly*. Which words relate in the same way?

   bird : butterfly

   Ⓐ seal : bear

   Ⓑ giraffe : monkey

   Ⓒ tiger : lion

   Ⓓ goat : mountain

4. Jenn wants to see Africa. She will see

   Ⓐ monkeys

   Ⓑ bears

   Ⓒ goats

   Ⓓ cats

5. The bears are next to the seals. They are

   Ⓐ making a home

   Ⓑ after the seals

   Ⓒ far away

   Ⓓ close by the seals

Walking to School

These are new words to practice.
Say each word 10 times.

✳ corner	✳ railroad
✳ station	✳ flag
✳ key	✳ cross
✳ sidewalk	✳ guard

Choose one new word to write.

_____

- -

_____

114

Walking to School

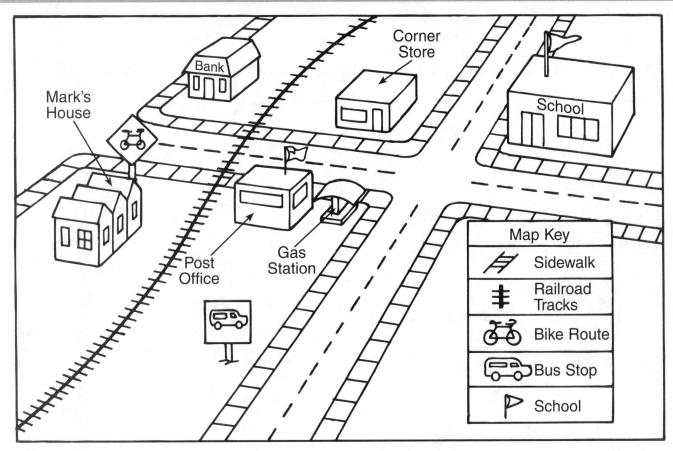

Every day Mark walks to school. He walks to the corner. He crosses the street. He walks across the railroad tracks.

Soon Mark sees the flag. He is almost to school.

Mark stops at the next corner. A crossing guard helps the children. They cross the street to go to school.

Walking to School

Look at the picture on page 115. Read the story.
Use the picture and the story to answer the questions.

1. This story is mainly about

   Ⓐ how to take the bus

   Ⓑ how to ride a bike

   Ⓒ how Mark gets to school

   Ⓓ how to cross the street

2. The *crossing guard*

   Ⓐ watches children to keep them safe

   Ⓑ barks at the children

   Ⓒ keeps children from running away

   Ⓓ protects the children with a cross

3. Think about how the word *sidewalk* relates to the word *street*. Which words relate in the same way?

   | **sidewalk : street** |

   Ⓐ map : key

   Ⓑ walk : cross

   Ⓒ bank : school

   Ⓓ railroad tracks : bike route

4. Which statement is true?

   Ⓐ The crossing guard is by Mark's house.

   Ⓑ The school has a flag.

   Ⓒ Mark waits at the bus stop.

   Ⓓ Mark walks on the bike route.

5. Mark walks past the

   Ⓐ bank

   Ⓑ pet store

   Ⓒ bus stop

   Ⓓ gas station

Checking the Weather

These are new words to practice.
Say each word 10 times.

* north
* legend

* east
* cloudy

* south
* windy

* west
* weather

Choose one new word to write.

_____

– – – – – – – – – – – – – – – – – – – –

_____

Checking the Weather

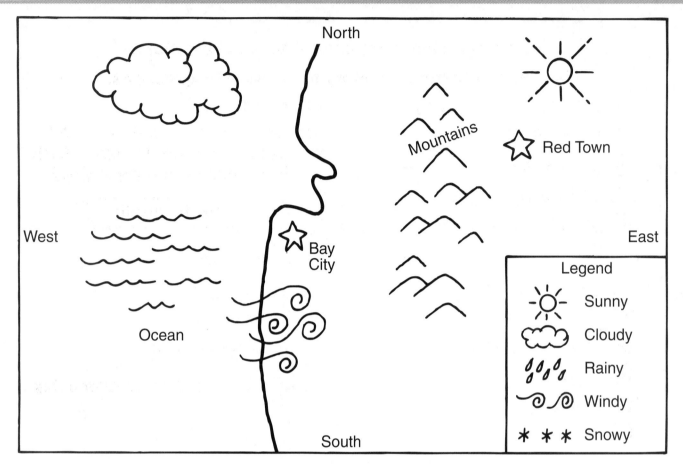

Dave lives in Bay City. His friend Al lives in Red Town. Dave wants to see Al.

Dave's dad checks the weather. Will it snow on the way to Al's house? Dave looks at today's weather map.

The weather looks good. It might rain. It will not snow. Dave can go see Al.

Checking the Weather

Look at the picture on page 118. Read the story.

Use the picture and the story to answer the questions.

1. When the wind blows

   Ⓐ you get wet

   Ⓑ you can feel air move

   Ⓒ you feel warm or hot

   Ⓓ you are next to the ocean

2. Dave cannot see Al if the weather is

   Ⓐ sunny

   Ⓑ windy

   Ⓒ snowy

   Ⓓ cloudy

3. This story is mainly about

   Ⓐ the weather

   Ⓑ Dave and Al

   Ⓒ Al's house

   Ⓓ the ocean

4. Think about how the word *north* relates to the word *south*. Which words relate in the same way?

north : south

   Ⓐ rain : clouds

   Ⓑ sun : snow

   Ⓒ east : west

   Ⓓ wind : weather

5. Al has this kind of *weather* at his house

   Ⓐ cloudy

   Ⓑ rainy

   Ⓒ windy

   Ⓓ sunny

A Trip to the Fish Hatchery

These are new words to practice.

Say each word 10 times.

* salmon   * hatchery

* trout   * display

* information   * guide

* booth   * bridge

Choose one new word to write.

_____

- -

_____

A Trip to the Fish Hatchery

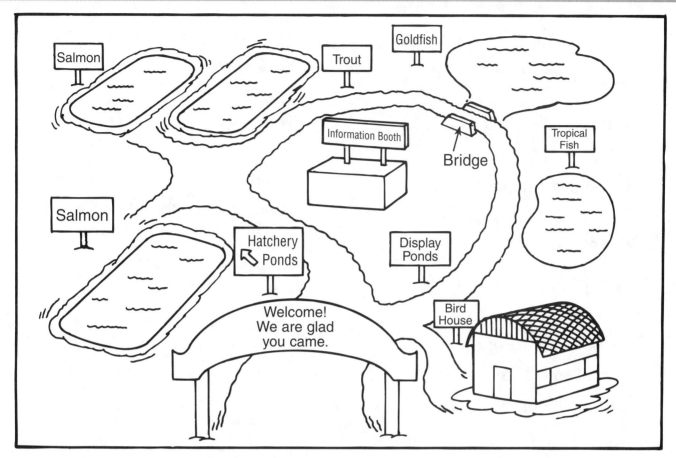

Meg's class is going on a field trip. They will go to the fish hatchery. They will see many things.

Meg's class goes to the hatchery ponds first. A guide tells the class about the fish.

One pond has baby fish in it. They feed the fish two times a day.

The class walks to the display ponds. They cross the bridge.

Meg likes the tropical fish. She sees many bright colors.

It is time to go back to school. The class will not see the bird house. Meg learned new things on the field trip.

A Trip to the Fish Hatchery

Look at the picture on page 121. Read the story.

Use the picture and the story to answer the questions.

1. Meg can find goldfish

   Ⓐ in the bird house

   Ⓑ in the hatchery ponds

   Ⓒ in the display ponds

   Ⓓ at the information booth

2. This story is mainly about

   Ⓐ a bird house

   Ⓑ a fish hatchery

   Ⓒ a fish display

   Ⓓ a field trip

3. Meg has a question about fish. She can

   Ⓐ ask her teacher

   Ⓑ read the map

   Ⓒ look at the fish

   Ⓓ go to the information booth

4. The *guide*

   Ⓐ shows Meg's class the fish hatchery

   Ⓑ helps the class across the bridge

   Ⓒ hatches baby fish

   Ⓓ feeds the birds

5. Think about how the word *fish* relates to the word *pond*. Which words relate in the same way?

fish : pond

   Ⓐ hatchery : guide

   Ⓑ bird : nest

   Ⓒ bridge : booth

   Ⓓ trout : salmon

Happy Birthday

These are new words to practice.

Say each word 10 times.

✳ card   ✳ unwrap

✳ present   ✳ balloon

✳ party   ✳ cake

✳ wrap   ✳ ice cream

Choose one new word to write.

_____

- -

_____

Happy Birthday

Today is Karl's birthday. He will get cards. He will get presents. There will be a party.

Karl opens this card. He reads the card. He likes the sun on the front.

Karl unwraps presents. He tears the wrapping paper.

There are balloons at the party. Karl eats cake and ice cream. He has fun at his party.

Happy Birthday

Look at the picture on page 124. Read the story.

Use the picture and the story to answer the questions.

1. This picture is mainly about

    (A) cake and ice cream

    (B) a birthday party

    (C) birthday presents

    (D) a birthday card

2. Karl's dad hopes Karl will

    (A) have fun on his birthday

    (B) eat ice cream on his birthday

    (C) be good on his birthday

    (D) play in the sun

3. Karl will *unwrap presents*. He will

    (A) cut the box

    (B) take off the outside paper

    (C) cover them with paper

    (D) untie the string

4. Think about how the word *wrap* relates to the word *unwrap*. Which words relate in the same way?

wrap : unwrap

    (A) cake : ice cream

    (B) birthday : presents

    (C) open : close

    (D) balloons : streamers

5. Karl got this card from

    (A) his father

    (B) his uncle

    (C) his mother

    (D) his friend

New Year's Day

These are new words to practice.

Say each word 10 times.

✳ celebrate	✳ parade
✳ confetti	✳ watch
✳ horn	✳ march
✳ honk	✳ float

Choose one new word to write.

_____

- - - - - - - - - - - - - - - - - - - -

_____

New Year's Day

Daily News

January 1, 2007

People Celebrate!

Last night we started a new year.

People threw confetti. They blew paper horns.

Car horns honked.

The parade is today. Watch it on TV at 9:00 a.m.

Happy New Year!

This morning Nick brought in the newspaper. He saw a picture. People were wearing party hats.

The people marched in a parade. Some people rode in old cars.

Other people sat on floats. The floats had many flowers.

Nick wants to see the parade. He will watch it on TV.

He gets his paper horn. Nick will celebrate the new year!

New Year's Day

Look at the picture on page 127. Read the story.

Use the picture and the story to answer the questions.

1. When you *celebrate* a holiday, you might

   Ⓐ sing a song

   Ⓑ eat dinner

   Ⓒ have a party

   Ⓓ sell something

2. People threw

   Ⓐ cars

   Ⓑ flowers

   Ⓒ confetti

   Ⓓ horns

3. This story is mainly about

   Ⓐ how people celebrate a new year

   Ⓑ how to be in a parade

   Ⓒ how to blow a horn

   Ⓓ how to throw confetti

4. Why does Nick have a paper horn?

   Ⓐ to look at

   Ⓑ to celebrate the new year

   Ⓒ to write on

   Ⓓ to be in a band

5. Think about how the word *throw* relates to the word *confetti*. Which words relate in the same way?

throw : confetti

   Ⓐ float : flowers

   Ⓑ honk : horn

   Ⓒ new : year

   Ⓓ parade : march

128   ©*Teacher Created Resources, Inc.*

Valentine's Day

These are new words to practice.
Say each word 10 times.

❋ valentine	❋ heart
❋ punch	❋ candy
❋ decorate	❋ sweet
❋ friend	❋ sticker

Choose one new word to write.

- -

Valentine's Day

Miss Timm decorates the classroom. She puts up paper hearts. The children help her.

The class plans a party. They want to have sweets.

They will have apples. They will have candy hearts. They will have fruit punch.

Ruth makes valentines. She makes one for each person. She puts a sticker on each one.

Valentine's Day

Look at the picture on page 130. Read the story.

Use the picture and the story to answer the questions.

1. What will the children do at the party?

   Ⓐ make valentines

   Ⓑ hand out valentines

   Ⓒ make holders for valentines

   Ⓓ decorate the classroom

2. This story is mainly about

   Ⓐ candy

   Ⓑ friends

   Ⓒ hearts

   Ⓓ a party

3. Think about how the word *candy* relates to the word *heart*. Which words relate in the same way?

candy : heart

   Ⓐ sticker : card

   Ⓑ valentine : party

   Ⓒ fruit : punch

   Ⓓ apples : sweet

4. A *valentine* is

   Ⓐ a card you give to a friend

   Ⓑ a heart on the wall

   Ⓒ a sticker on your desk

   Ⓓ a candy heart

5. Miss Timm put up hearts in the classroom. The hearts are most likely

   Ⓐ white and purple

   Ⓑ red and yellow

   Ⓒ pink and red

   Ⓓ purple and blue

Fourth of July

These are new words to practice.

Say each word 10 times.

✻ Independence Day   ✻ picnic

✻ fireworks   ✻ holiday

✻ sparkler   ✻ color

✻ band   ✻ noise

Choose one new word to write.

_____

- -

_____

Fourth of July

Trey and Faith went to the park. They went with their family. They will have a picnic.

Today is a holiday. It is a special day. Many things will take place at the park.

Trey can buy a hot dog. It is hot off the grill.

Faith asks her dad to buy sparklers. They have many colors. They make a little noise.

Trey and Faith think the Fourth of July is a great day!

Fourth of July

Look at the picture on page 133. Read the story.

Use the picture and the story to answer the questions.

1. This story is mainly about

   (A) the hot dog stand

   (B) the band concert

   (C) the Fourth of July

   (D) the fireworks show

2. Independence Day is on

   (A) the 3rd Saturday in July

   (B) the 4th of July

   (C) the 1st of July

   (D) the 2nd of June

3. If Trey has a *picnic*, he will

   (A) eat outside

   (B) pick flowers

   (C) play outside

   (D) watch a parade

4. Think about how the word *sparklers* relates to the word *color*. Which words relate in the same way?

   sparklers : color

   (A) band : concert

   (B) fireworks : noise

   (C) hot dog : grill

   (D) picnic : table

5. Faith's dad can buy sparklers for

   (A) $30

   (B) $2

   (C) $5

   (D) $3

134

A Thanksgiving Feast

These are new words to practice.
Say each word 10 times.

✳ feast	✳ pumpkin
✳ Pilgrim	✳ grateful
✳ thanks	✳ harvest
✳ turkey	✳ American Indian

Choose one new word to write.

_____

- -

_____

A Thanksgiving Feast

It is November. Brad has a page to color. It is about Thanksgiving.

Brad reads the words aloud. He colors the pictures. Brad's class talks about Thanksgiving.

Brad likes this day. He eats good food. He spends time with his family.

A Thanksgiving Feast

Look at the picture on page 135. Read the story.

Use the picture and the story to answer the questions.

1. The Pilgrims gave thanks for the harvest. They were *grateful* for

   Ⓐ the farm

   Ⓑ the food they could grow

   Ⓒ warm weather

   Ⓓ their family

2. The words in the picture tell

   Ⓐ about the first Thanksgiving

   Ⓑ what colors to use

   Ⓒ a story

   Ⓓ what the words mean

3. This story is mainly about

   Ⓐ a feast

   Ⓑ Pilgrims

   Ⓒ family

   Ⓓ pumpkin pie

4. Thanksgiving is a holiday in

   Ⓐ December

   Ⓑ October

   Ⓒ November

   Ⓓ June

5. Think about how the word *read* relates to the word *word*. Which words relate in the same way?

read : word

   Ⓐ color : picture

   Ⓑ bird : turkey

   Ⓒ corn : pumpkin

   Ⓓ November : Thanksgiving

Winter Holidays

These are new words to practice.

Say each word 10 times.

✳ wreath	✳ tree
✳ lights	✳ candle
✳ festival	✳ star
✳ gift	✳ special

Choose one new word to write.

_____

- -

_____

Winter Holidays

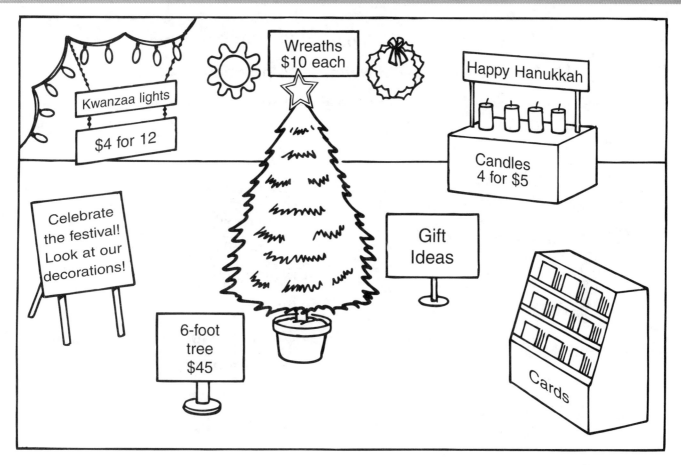

Gail went to the store with her mom. The store had many things.

Gail saw holiday decorations. She saw a star on a tree.

They looked at the wreaths. Gail's mom got a card. Gail got a gift for her sister.

Gail will celebrate the holidays with her family. They will put up lights. They will eat special food. Gail is excited about the holidays!

Winter Holidays

Quiz

Look at the picture on page 139. Read the story.

Use the picture and the story to answer the questions.

1. For which holidays is the store decorated?

    Ⓐ Hanukkah, Kwanzaa

    Ⓑ Christmas, New Year's

    Ⓒ Christmas, Hanukkah, Kwanzaa

    Ⓓ Christmas, Hanukkah, New Year's

2. This story is mainly about

    Ⓐ special food

    Ⓑ winter holidays

    Ⓒ gifts

    Ⓓ lights

3. Think about how the word *candle* relates to the word *light*. Which words relate in the same way?

    candle : light

    Ⓐ tree : green

    Ⓑ special : gift

    Ⓒ wreath : star

    Ⓓ card : holiday

4. A *festival* is a type of

    Ⓐ holiday

    Ⓑ celebrate

    Ⓒ special day

    Ⓓ day with family

5. Gail could find a card for her friend

    Ⓐ on the left side of the store

    Ⓑ by the lights

    Ⓒ in the back of the store

    Ⓓ at the front of the store

Answer Sheets

Student Name

Title of Reading Passage

1. (a) (b) (c) (d)
2. (a) (b) (c) (d)
3. (a) (b) (c) (d)
4. (a) (b) (c) (d)
5. (a) (b) (c) (d)

Student Name

Title of Reading Passage

1. (a) (b) (c) (d)
2. (a) (b) (c) (d)
3. (a) (b) (c) (d)
4. (a) (b) (c) (d)
5. (a) (b) (c) (d)

Student Name

Title of Reading Passage

1. (a) (b) (c) (d)
2. (a) (b) (c) (d)
3. (a) (b) (c) (d)
4. (a) (b) (c) (d)
5. (a) (b) (c) (d)

Student Name

Title of Reading Passage

1. (a) (b) (c) (d)
2. (a) (b) (c) (d)
3. (a) (b) (c) (d)
4. (a) (b) (c) (d)
5. (a) (b) (c) (d)

Vocabulary List

able	clue	gift	office	sidewalk
across	collar	giraffe	open	sign
Africa	color	glass	order	silent
afternoon	comb	grade	over	slip
again	computer	grain	pack	snack
age	concert	grateful	paper	soap
aloud	confetti	grocery	parade	social studies
American Indian	connect	group	party	sort
animal	control	guard	patch	south
answer	copy	guess	path	sparkler
appointment	corner	gym	patient	special
area	correct	hand cleanser	permission	split
arrow	counter	hand soap	pet	sport
ask	crayons	harvest	picnic	squeeze
attack	cross	heart	picture	stack
aunt	crosswalk	help	piece	star
back	cup	helper	Pilgrim	start
balloon	cursor	holiday	pitcher	station
band	customer	honk	plan	stay
basket	daily	hope	plastic	sticker
bin	danger	horn	play	stop light
blow	deck	hours	playground	store
bookcase	decorate	ice	please	stove
boots	defense	ice cream	point	student
bought	dentist	icon	pour	sugar
breakfast	describe	Independence Day	practice	sweep
bring	directions	insert	present	sweet
broken	dish soap	invitation	printed	task
broom	disk	item	prize	team
brush	doctor	job	produce	test
busy	door	journal	protect	thanks
button	dresser	key	pull	tie
cake	duck	kit	pumpkin	toothbrush
calendar	DVD	kitchen	punch	toothpaste
candle	east	leash	push	towel
candles	enemy	legend	railroad	tree
candy	enjoy	lemon	ready	trip
card	enter	lemonade	recess	turkey
cartoon	escape	library	recipe	turn
caution	events	lights	recycle	uncle
celebrate	exchange	lotion	remote control	unwrap
cereal	exit	male	return	valentine
channel	favorite	map	right	value
character	feast	march	route	vitamins
chart	female	meal	rules	wait
checkout	festival	men	safety	walk
cheese	fetch	menu	sale	warning
chew	field trip	morning	sandwich	watch
choose	find	movie	schedule	weather
chores	finish	napkin	score	west
classroom	fireworks	new	screen	win
click	flag	newspaper	seal	window
close	flea	next	sell	windy
closed	float	noise	serving	women
closet	friend	north	set	wrap
clothes	game	noun	shake	wreath
cloudy	garbage	nuggets	shampoo	write
club	garden	object	show	yesterday

     142   ©Teacher Created Resources, Inc.

Answer Key

Page 11—Kala Helps Her Mom
1. C
2. A
3. C
4. D
5. B

Page 14—Buying a Newspaper
1. C
2. A
3. D
4. B
5. A

Page 17—Seth's Lunch
1. B
2. D
3. C
4. D
5. A

Page 20—Sam Goes Shopping
1. B
2. C
3. D
4. A
5. B

Page 23—Snack Time
1. B
2. D
3. C
4. A
5. B

Page 26—Hana Goes to the Dentist
1. A
2. B
3. C
4. A
5. D

Page 29—Lian's New Coloring Book
1. C
2. A
3. B
4. D
5. A

Page 32—Flowers
1. C
2. A
3. B
4. D
5. B

Page 35—Reading Directions
1. A
2. C
3. B
4. D
5. A

Page 38—Taking a Test
1. D
2. A
3. A
4. B
5. C

Page 41—Making a Caterpillar
1. D
2. B
3. C
4. A
5. B

Page 44—The Pumpkin Patch
1. B
2. C
3. D
4. A
5. B

Page 47—Helping in the Kitchen
1. A
2. C
3. B
4. D
5. B

Page 50—Circus Crunch
1. D
2. B
3. A
4. C
5. B

Page 53—Tim Takes Care of His Puppy
1. A
2. D
3. C
4. B
5. A

Page 56—Recycle Day
1. C
2. C
3. C
4. D
5. B

Page 59—Packing for a Trip
1. C
2. A
3. B
4. B
5. D

Page 62—The Lemonade Stand
1. C
2. A
3. C
4. D
5. B

Page 65—Saturday Cleaning
1. B
2. D
3. A
4. C
5. B

Page 68—June Fun
1. B
2. C
3. D
4. A
5. C

Page 71—Come to the Party
1. A
2. C
3. B
4. B
5. D

Page 74—Maki's Day at School
1. B
2. A
3. D
4. C
5. B

Page 77—Day Camp
1. B
2. A
3. C
4. A
5. D

Page 80—Ben's Chores
1. B
2. C
3. D
4. B
5. D

Answer Key *(cont.)*

Page 83—What Is on TV?

1. A
2. B
3. C
4. B
5. D

Page 86—Guess My Game

1. C
2. A
3. D
4. C
5. B

Page 89—People, Places, and Things

1. B
2. D
3. A
4. D
5. C

Page 92—Summer Camp

1. A
2. C
3. B
4. D
5. A

Page 95—Grandma's House

1. B
2. A
3. C
4. B
5. D

Page 98—Kip and Kyle

1. C
2. B
3. A
4. B
5. A

Page 101—Say, Do

1. C
2. D
3. A
4. C
5. B

Page 106—Jean Goes to the Park

1. C
2. A
3. B
4. C
5. A

Page 107—Fire Safety Plan

1. A
2. D
3. C
4. C
5. B

Page 110—Kay's New School

1. D
2. B
3. A
4. C
5. B

Page 113—Around the Zoo

1. B
2. A
3. C
4. A
5. D

Page 116—Walking to School

1. C
2. A
3. D
4. B
5. A

Page 119—Checking the Weather

1. B
2. C
3. A
4. C
5. D

Page 122—A Trip to the Fish Hatchery

1. C
2. B
3. D
4. A
5. B

Page 125—Happy Birthday

1. D
2. A
3. B
4. C
5. A

Page 128—New Year's Day

1. C
2. C
3. A
4. B
5. B

Page 131—Valentine's Day

1. B
2. D
3. C
4. A
5. C

Page 134—Fourth of July

1. C
2. B
3. A
4. B
5. D

Page 137—A Thanksgiving Feast

1. B
2. A
3. A
4. C
5. A

Page 140—Winter Holidays

1. C
2. B
3. C
4. A
5. D